PRAISE FOR *HIRING RIGHT*

"Hiring Right *is an indispensable business book, the complete guide to how to hire the best people for your business at any given time. Bolaji Olagunju has decades of business and recruitment experience and puts it to great use in a manual that is practical, insightful and humorous. I'd highly recommend this to anyone who is ever going to need to hire staff."*

Hugh Barker

Author, *Million Dollar Maths*

"Do you keep hiring the 'wrong' people? Hiring Right *is the book for you. Concise and jargon-free, it lists the ten biggest mistakes that organisations make in this area and comes up with clear, practical answers to each of them. The author is a top HR professional, who has seen all sides of the employment story, as an employee, as a consultant and as an employer, and has learnt from his experiences in all of them. However large or small your organisation, this book will enable you to get the right people onboard and to keep them motivated."*

Chris West

Co-author, *The Beermat Entrepreneur*

"Buy this book. Buy it now. Study it. Get everybody involved in hiring on behalf of your organization to read it. It might just be the difference-maker between failure and spectacular success."*

Nweike Onwuyali
CEO, Esofties Technologies

"Excellent and well written. Hiring Right *is easy to read and relate with as a business executive quickly bringing into sharp focus the real life challenges faced in building a sustainable and successful business. Bolaji's experience as a thorough-bred professional in the HR space comes through clearly and his unique insights as a business owner and executive provides the much needed balance that makes Hiring Right such a pragmatic read. I recommend the book as must-have for senior managers and persons responsible for hiring in any organization. And the recommendations and practices are must-dos for serious minded executives and business people."*

Obinnia Abajue
CEO, Hygeia HMO

"Unlike many books I have come across in this genre, this book is written by someone who has lived and breathed the principles of hiring right … Bolaji Olagunju offers practical insights and guidance on how to hire the right people for your organizational success and continuity."

Rita Smith
Director, Orbit Solutions

"Hiring Right *is like an MBA in building a successful organization: an advanced course on how to design, develop and deploy the right approaches to finding and keeping the right people who will make the biggest difference in your business success."*

Elizabeth Bell
Co-founder, Lift Marketing

HIRING

RIGHT

BOLAJI OLAGUNJU

HIRING RIGHT

A MATTER OF LIFE AND DEATH FOR BUSINESSES, BUSINESS OWNERS AND EXECUTIVES

BOLAJI OLAGUNJU

FOUNDER, WORKFORCE GROUP

www.workforcegroup.com

Copyright

Cover Designer: Kofo Adesanya

Interior Designer: meadencreative.com

Cartoon Illustrator: Canary Pete

Hardcover ISBN: 978-1-7339779-9-9

Tradepaper ISBN: 978-1-7339779-8-2

Digital ISBN: 978-1-7339779-7-5

First edition, August 2019

This book is dedicated to my late Dad,
Michael Adeboye Olagunju
The most tolerant, compassionate, and fun
person I have ever known.

Daddy, my biggest regret in life is that you didn't live long enough to see your predictions about me come true. To this day, I am still striving to measure up to your high expectations of me. Sometimes, I wonder what made you believe so much in me. It's indeed a mystery, but I am glad you did as your belief continues to serve as a motivation to keep striving to be the best you said I could be.

CONTENTS

ACKNOWLEDGMENTS

I want to acknowledge my darling wife, Aderonke, for her love and support. Without it, this book would not have seen the light of day. Thank you for being there always. You make me want to be a better version of myself.

To my colleagues at Workforce Group, thank you for all your dedication, support and commitment for what we do and what we stand for as a company. You all inspire me.

Special acknowledgment goes to Foluso Aribisala for steadying the ship while I was mostly away trying to write this book amongst other things. Your loyalty and commitment are deeply humbling.

To all our clients too numerous to mention, this book would not have been possible without the opportunity to work with and learn from you. My association with you has been truly enriching. I simply cannot thank you enough.

To my mum, thank you for your special love and care for me, and for always tolerating my excesses. And for sitting on a stool in front of my room for hours on end...

To my friends, Alex, Obinnia, Dapo, Nweike, Dele, Kola, Uvie and Dayo thanks for always being there. Your support and encouragement mean a lot.

To my publishing team, Elizabeth, Chris, Honoree, Kofo, Barry, Hugh and Andy, thank you for your hard work and dedication to ensuring that this book came into reality. I am very grateful for all your help.

Last but not the least, to my amazing children, Oluwatomilola, Ibukunoluwa, Oluwapoju and Oluwapelumi, my desire to inspire you to greatness and be the right model for you all keeps me going. If I can do this, you can do so much more with your God-given potentials.

INTRODUCTION

I completely disagree with and unequivocally reject the notion that people are the greatest asset an organization can possess. As a matter of fact, nothing can be farther from the truth. A more realistic view is this: People can potentially be the biggest liability an organization can have.

From my years of experience as a business executive and advisor to several businesses from startups to high-growth companies and large established corporations, I can categorically say that the more people an organization has to manage, the higher the likelihood that potential problems for the organization will arise. Of course, many employees are likely to disagree with this statement, but unfortunately, it is the truth.

If you share this view with employers, business owners, and executives, I am positive that the majority of them will not only be in agreement but will also have battle scars, war stories, and undesirable experiences to share regarding the devastating impact people can have on a business.

On the other hand, it is an undeniable fact that the right people are by far the greatest asset an organization can possess. In over two decades of helping organizations improve their business performance, I have personally experienced and observed many mind-boggling accounts of the sheer amount of value that can be created by having the right people within an organization. Make no mistake about it: Having the right people makes all the difference when it comes to the success and business continuity of any organization.

My organization and our numerous clients' businesses would not be where they are today without the competence, commitment and contribution of the right people. The right people can transform the fortunes of an organization, helping it to create and capture immeasurable market value. So much so, that I am convinced that it is practically impossible to quantify the true value of the right people accurately.

In essence, people can potentially be the biggest liability or the difference maker. Herein, lies one of the biggest paradoxes in business. And as with most paradoxes, thriving and survival require that you do everything you can to ensure you're on the right side and that you possess in-depth knowledge of what to do to take advantage of, and benefit immensely from the situation.

Years of experience spent helping organizations build the requisite capability and acquire the right to win in their market place has taught me that nothing an organization does can be more important than hiring the right people. Absolutely nothing!

Hiring right is literally a matter of life and death for business owners, executives, and their organizations. Businesses have died because of wrong hiring decisions. Business owners have lost everything—their health, their relationship and even their lives—because of wrong hiring decisions.

The Greatest and Worst Hiring Decisions Ever

As a recruiter and CEO, who has personally experienced as well as witnessed several value-creating hiring decisions and devastating, value-destroying ones, I have often pondered the question of which hiring decisions will go down in the hall of fame as the greatest and worst hiring choices ever.

Tony Hsieh, CEO of online shoe and clothing retailer Zappos, reckons that he has lost £76m to bad hires. But even that pales into insignificance beside the worst hiring decision ever…

I recently asked a room full of 87 business executives at a Digital Technology Conference to share the greatest and worst hiring decisions in the course of their career and to vote for what they believed was the greatest and worst hiring decision of all time.

While some of them shared awe-inspiring tales of value-creating hiring decisions, most of the stories, unfortunately, were horrific tales of hiring decisions gone wrong.

However, everyone in the group agreed that the greatest hiring decision of all time had to be that of the board of Apple to re-hire Steve Jobs as CEO in 1997 even though at the time it was regarded as an interim position. This single hiring decision led to value creation of unimaginable proportions.

At the beginning of Jobs's second reign, in 1997, Apple's market capitalization was approximately $3 billion. By 2011, Apple had surpassed Exxon Mobil Corp as the largest corporation in the United States, with a market capitalization of $355 billion. He resigned in 2011 as CEO but, based on his influence and impact, Apple Inc. rose to become the first trillion-dollar company in the world. Very few business leaders have had as dramatic an influence on multiple industries as Steve Jobs did to the computer, music, mobile and movie industries.

What about the vote for the worst hiring decision?

While the choice of Steve Jobs for the best hiring decision had been unanimous, there was some debate about the worst, with two of the executives present at the conference insisting their own negative hiring experiences were unmatched.

Finally, after much debate, the group settled on Nick Leeson, the rogue trader who single-handedly caused the collapse of Barings, the United Kingdom's oldest merchant bank, in 1995. Through fraudulent, unauthorized and speculative trading activities he managed to lose the bank £825 million, after which the once-thriving company was sold to a rival for a nominal price of £1.

According to one CEO in the discussion, what made this the worst hiring decision ever was not just the loss but the fact that the rogue trader went on to become a celebrity after causing the collapse of the bank, devastating shareholders and causing thousands to lose their source of livelihood. His story was later made into a movie and he travels all over the world giving keynote addresses and speeches about his exploits, even appearing on UK reality TV show Celebrity Big Brother.

But, hiring right isn't just about choosing the right leader. Andrew Carnegie, who built the world's first £1 billion company, US Steel, in the late nineteenth century, clearly appreciated the importance of hiring right: he even had this message written on his tombstone:

Here lies a man
Who knew how to enlist
In his service
Better men than himself

Even in death, the great businessman wanted the world to know that the most important thing a business executive could do was to do everything, short of crime and sin, to ensure they hire the right people. It is an inscription that sums up the entire premise of this book.

This epitaph is such a powerful illustration of the importance of hiring right. I believe most business executives will benefit immensely from adopting a similar philosophy with respect to how they lead and manage their organizations.

Wrong Hiring Is a Lose-Lose Proposition

"If you hire well, the benefits are multiplied and seem nearly endless. If you hire poorly, the problems are multiplied and seem endless."

David Forman

I have experienced first-hand the devastating effect of wrong hiring on business owners, senior executives, managers, customers, communities and, sadly, even a nation. Wrong hiring is a zero-sum game. When an organization fails to consistently hire right, everyone loses:

Customers

The biggest losers are often the innocent customers of organizations that consistently make wrong hiring decisions. Through no fault of theirs, they have to endure horrendously poor services, failed promises, financial losses, and many other unfair and too-numerous-to-mention unpleasant experiences.

The Manager of the Wrong Hire.

The second biggest loser is the manager of the "unfit" employee who is likely to end up with a "paid audience," an employee who watches the manager do the work he or she is being paid to do. Many managers are stressed out and overwhelmed because of the poor quality of the employees working under them. How on earth can a manager be strategic in their role (something that is critical to their success) when they spend most of their time reworking the sub-standard work outputs of their direct reports?

The Wrong Hire

Hiring an employee for a position they are not a "fit" for is unfair to that person, too. I believe that every employee wants to succeed in his or her job. They want to be recognized for an exceptional performance. They want to be able to take pride and joy in their work and to feel fulfilled. Hiring employees for roles they aren't suited for can have devastatingly adverse effects on them. Their self-esteem can take a significant hit, leading to depression, which can spread to every aspect of their lives: health, wellbeing, relationship, and family.

Colleagues of the Wrong Hire

There is nothing more damaging to team spirit and collegial relationships than colleagues who are weak links. Work is tough enough without having to do other people's work in addition to one's own. Weak links have a divisive effect on a team's morale and productivity.

Other People in the Organization

Wrong hires deprive everyone in the organization of important advancement opportunities, clogging the organization up with immovable "deadwood." They can create a downward spiral, in which the best employees look around at the poor hires being made and decide to jump ship because they want to work alongside competent people in a more stimulating environment. If these top-quality leavers are then replaced by poor fits, things can go from bad to worse.

The Organization Itself

In addition to the obvious short-term financial loss caused by under-performance, the company will suffer damage to long-term intangible assets like morale, reputation and creativity.

CASE STUDY

Whose Fault is it?

When I find an employee who turns out to be wrong for a job, I feel it is my fault because I made the decision to hire him."

Akio Morita

My firm recently offered business advisory services to a company that was almost dead. The situation we met on ground was so bad that I felt particularly sorry for the CEO, who was also the founder and majority shareholder.

Years of wrong hiring decisions had caught up with them and this was taking its toll on the business and its executives. In all my years of providing advisory services to business executives, I am yet to meet a more tired, worn-out, unhealthy, and generally burnt-out group of executives.

The team supporting them was so weak that the executives were working up to 18 hours a day just to keep the business from going under. Sadly, most of their time was spent firefighting and reworking the poor quality work their direct reports had done.

A diagnostic exercise revealed that the company had broken all the rules regarding hiring right. They had made every single hiring mistake covered in this book and then some: including a few that are just too embarrassing to share in this book.

During the briefing session at which we presented the report, the executives began pointing fingers at their direct reports and complaining bitterly about the quality of their workforce. This went on and on until I couldn't stand it any longer and decided to shock them into reality by sharing this famous hiring quote with them:

Who exactly is the idiot? The idiot who was hired or the idiot who hired the idiot?"

That got their attention. For about a minute, there was a deathly silence in the room as the reality of what I just said sunk in. After the awkward silence, I was able to refocus the conversation on how to move forward and turn the situation around.

It took a while to change the status quo; it was a tough task and a roller coaster journey. At some points, I thought the executives weren't going to make it because they were so exhausted and experiencing burn out. But they somehow managed to pull through, thanks to their commitment, sheer determination and willingness to dig deep to find the strength to push through the transformation effort needed to resuscitate the company.

Within eighteen months, they had renewed and revamped the organization, replacing most of the wrong hires with the right people.

Why is Wrong Hiring so Prevalent in Organizations?

It is a proven fact that the companies with the best people are the most consistent business winners. Most businesses and their executives know the critical importance of hiring right. However, more often than not, *that knowledge doesn't necessarily translate into action.*

Why is this so?

According to a 2017 Harris Poll survey, seventy-four percent of the 2257 hiring managers and HR professionals surveyed admitted that they have "often" made wrong hires. It has been estimated that a wrongly hired line manager with a salary of £42,000 costs an organization £132,015 in wasted salary, recruiting and training fees, personal productivity, team productivity and staff turnover.

Why do highly intelligent, driven, and rational business owners/ executives continue to make wrong hiring decisions that place lids on the vast potential of their business enterprise and jeopardize their success and even continued survival? What are the reasons why organizations struggle or fail outright in their bid to consistently hire the right people for their company's context and situation? Also, what are the practical steps business owners and executives can take to significantly increase their probability of successfully hiring the right people?

From my twenty years of training and developing hiring managers, teaching them how to consistently make the right hires, as well as my experiences of hiring for my own businesses, I have identified the following top ten reasons why organizations fail to hire right:

1   Failure to understand and align with organizational context
2   Absence of clearly defined and documented hiring process
3   Failure to develop and use Success Profiles in the hiring process
4   Untrained interviewers or recruiters
5   Hiring biases
6   Relying on interviews and not using a variety of assessment methodologies in the hiring process
7   Lack of clear accountability
8   Poor allocation of resources
9   Failing to deal with the issues raised by the talent shortage
10 Murphy's Law

The rest of this book is organized into ten chapters based on this list: each describes the nature of the challenges faced and gives a practical guide to solving them. There will also be case studies to show these solutions in action.

> *If you hire the right people, you won't have problems later on. If you hire the wrong people, for whatever reason, you're in serious trouble, and all the revolutionary management techniques in the world may not bail you out."*
>
> **John Callos**

I wrote this book to serve as a practical guidebook to help organizations of all sizes and their executives succeed and thrive by hiring the right people for their context. Executives from large to high-growth as well as, startups will benefit significantly from this "view-from-the-trenches" of getting hiring practices right.

While this book is based on over two decades of professional experience of helping organizations with their hiring needs as well as training thousands of managers, it is also based on my personal experience of starting and running multiple businesses. It captures lessons learned, personal mistakes, and a collection of best practices in the field of hiring that has helped countless businesses, including mine, acquire the right to win in the marketplace.

In this book, I wear four different hats.

The first is that of a veteran business executive who has experienced the unmatched joy of getting hiring right and reaped the bountiful rewards, and one who has gotten it horribly wrong and paid the devastating price.

Veteran Business Executive

The second hat I'm wearing is that of a business consultant to some of the foremost and most interesting businesses in our market. I have made many mistakes including the ones I advise my clients not to make (I'm only human after all). I must add here that it has been a real privilege to have had the opportunity to work with and learn from so many intelligent business executives while being paid for my services.

Business Consultant

The third hat is that of an HR professional. I'm convinced that the most significant contribution my professional colleagues can make to their organizations is to ensure that they consistently attract, hire, and retain the right people for their particular situation or requirements. This is so important.

HR Professional

If there is one thing that is difficult to do, but if HR professionals can do it exceptionally well, will have the potential to transform the fortunes of their organisation, it is hiring right!

Finally, the fourth hat I wear is that of an investor. I have learnt the hard way that it is better to invest in the right team than in any product or business venture. This lesson is serving me extremely well in my new vocation of investing in and helping startups to go from scratch to scale.

Investor

In the course of reading the book, you may notice different biases based on these four roles, I apologize in advance if any of my biases contradicts the reader's point of view.

A Word of Caution on Business Growth

Growth is what most businesses desire, but it can be dangerous. Growth creates complexity, and complexity can be the biggest killer of growth. If you hire quickly but wrongly in the pursuit of growth, you are more likely than not to end up with a situation where your business experiences a decline—and you can even lose what you have previously built, leaving you worse off.

Whatever you do, you should never attempt to grow your business if you don't have enough of the right people. It's crucial to do everything possible to limit your growth based on your ability to hire the right people for your business. One of my favorite quotes on hiring is from Jim Collins, author of *Good to Great*. He said: "*A company should limit its growth based on its ability to find and keep enough of the right people.*"

Companies don't usually die of malnutrition—doing too little. They typically die of indigestion—doing too much.

Most companies erroneously believe that they have the right to grow just because they have brilliant ideas. The right to grow has to be earned and the starting point for this is hiring the right people for your business.

Are You Doing Your Best?

Sometimes I come across business executives who say they are "doing their best" in the area of hiring the right people for their organization. However, when I ask them to describe precisely what they are doing, they are unable to articulate their approaches. I typically say to them. What do you mean by saying you are doing your best? What if your best is not enough? What then?

In crucial matters of life and death like hiring right, simply believing that you are doing your best is just not good enough. You have to first find out what the best is and then do it.

Your organization (like mine) probably doesn't have a knowledge problem: we all know the importance of hiring the right people in theory. The problem is that we don't always convert that knowledge into practice: this book was written to help solve that problem.

Another word of caution: as you read the book, please do not say "I know this already." Instead, ask yourself if you are consistently practicing what you do know. As the saying goes: "The greatest gap in life (and business) is the gap between knowing and doing." You will do well by minding the knowing-doing gap in your hiring practice.

HIRING PRACTICES SCORE CARD

Before you dive into the book, take a moment to assess where your organization currently is relative to the Ten Hiring Mistakes covered in the book.

The Hiring Practices Scorecard was designed to serve as a guide that would help you identify the areas in which to focus your attention in order to achieve significant improvement in your hiring practices.

Use this tool to evaluate the effectiveness of your hiring processes and practices. For each of the items below, check the box that best describes your organization using the following key:

1 = Not at all

2 = To a small extent

3 = Somewhat

4 = To a large extent

5 = To a very great extent

1	We carry out detailed analysis of our organisational context and realities to determine the strategic implications on roles we are hiring for.	1 2 3 4 5
2	We have well developed Success Profiles for our critical roles and we deploy them as guides as part of our hiring activities.	1 2 3 4 5
3	We have clearly defined and documented hiring processes and practices that everyone with a hiring responsibility is required to follow diligently.	1 2 3 4 5
4	All our Hiring Managers, Recruiters, Interviewers and HR Staff are well trained and certified on our hiring processes and practices.	1 2 3 4 5
5	We recognise the potential negative impact of biases on our hiring activities and we have put in place adequate practices to eliminate biases, as much as possible, in our hiring practices.	1 2 3 4 5
6	We deploy a variety of candidate selection methodologies (at least 3) as part of our hiring process to increase our chances of hiring right.	1 2 3 4 5
7	We have set standards and metrics and we hold our hiring personnel accountable to them.	1 2 3 4 5
8	We provide adequate resources (budget, space, people, time) for all our hiring activities to ensure we get it right.	1 2 3 4 5
9	We have a strategy and implementation plan in place to grow our own talent to reduce the impact of talent shortage on our business.	1 2 3 4 5
10	We recognise that despite our best efforts, we can still experience failure in hiring right so we are productively paranoid and we do not leave anything to chance when it comes to our hiring process and practices.	1 2 3 4 5

Total Score: _____

Scoring Instructions: Add up the numeric value (1 to 5) of all the selected boxes. The maximum possible score is 50. Use the table below to assess the readiness of your hiring team to deliver the right people to support your business strategy and aspirations.

Points	Assessment Result
>45	Excellent likelihood of Hiring Right. Action: Continue a disciplined approach to improving your hiring practices; strengthen lowest-scoring items.
33-44	Moderate likelihood for hiring right, but results may be less than optimal. Action: Strengthen weakest items to raise the score to > 44.
<32	Hiring Right is less likely. Action: Urgently overhaul your entire hiring processes and practices in a systemic way.

CHAPTER ONE

CONTEXT IS EVERYTHING

"Always design a thing by considering it in its next larger context: a chair in a room, a room in a house, a house in an environment, an environment in a city plan."

Eliel Saarinen

One major lesson I've learned from more than twenty years of working and running businesses is this: when it comes to business management and organizational success, an understanding of context is essential. It is my firm conviction that the failure to understand this is one of the major reasons why organizations fail spectacularly, especially when it comes to hiring the right people.

According to the Merriam-Webster dictionary, "Context" now most commonly means *"The environment or setting in which something (whether words or events) exists."* When we say that something is contextualized, we mean that it is placed in an appropriate setting.

No two hiring briefs are the same, even for the same organization. The context of the organization must always be taken into due consideration for each hiring need.

There are various ways of modeling a business's context. One is a simple matrix of four types of contexts:

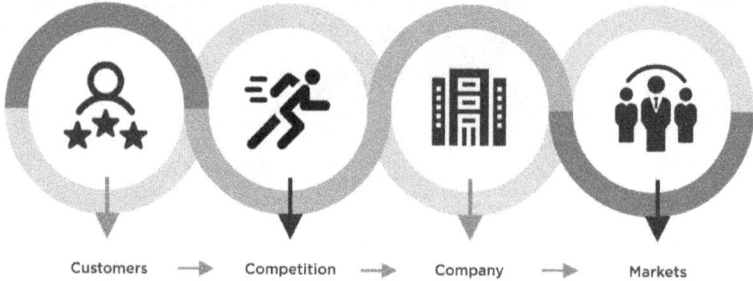

Customers → Competition → Company → Markets

This matrix is an extension of the 3Cs model of management guru Kenichi Ohmae, so we might call it the 3Cs + M model – a helpful extension in my view, firstly because it separates individual customers and their specific concerns (Customers) from general forces that affect the market as a whole (Market). Market, in turn, is often subdivided into "PESTLE" factors: political, economic, social, technological, legal, and environmental.

The model combines looking at the world out there with an internal focus on the third type of context: "Company". Your company has to be ready to meet the challenges posed by the other three factors in the model. And, of course, your company also has to be prepared to meet the challenges that are presented by your "Competition".

A company can only be effective and successful in achieving its desired goals and objectives to the degree to which it can brutally confront the realities of all these contexts and align its activities accordingly. To consistently hire right, an organization must ensure there is a "fit" between its business context and the people it is hiring. This is absolutely non-negotiable.

It is crucially important to understand that the "right person" for my organization might be the absolutely "wrong person" for your organization. Likewise, the "right person" for my organization today might be the "wrong person" for the organization in three to five years. There are no "wrong" people, just people out of context. When I talk of "wrong hires," this must always be borne in mind. I do not mean to casually write those people off altogether. Every person is valuable in their own right.

Having been privileged to have helped hundreds of organizations with their hiring needs, it never ceases to amaze me the degree to which the difference in the situation of the organization influences hiring decisions and their success or failure.

War and Peace

Another way of looking at organizational contexts is to think of "war" and "peace." These are two radically different sets of circumstances that confront businesses at one point or the other. In "war," businesses are fighting for their very survival. When they are at "peace" they are cruising, enjoying the momentum of success and taking maximum advantage of the growth opportunities available to them.

The types of people hired into these very different organizational contexts—even if they are operating in exactly the same industry—must be significantly different.

Organizations at war, fighting for their existence, need "Warrior CEO/ executives" and "Warrior employees." Anything short of this guarantees that the organization will struggle or even fail outright.

I have personally experienced wartime situations at least three different times in the course of running my businesses and on many more occasions while I was consulting for businesses that were fighting for their survival. Who you have on your team during this critical time will ultimately determine whether you will make it or not.

What are the key attributes of warriors?

They have great *resilience*. They have a "never say die" attitude. In the face of the most appalling difficulties, they press on, confident in their belief that they will ultimately prevail.

Warrior leaders *shield others*. They understand other people's fears and difficulties and help those people to stay strong and to keep the end in view.

They are brilliant *jugglers*. They are masters of complexity. In wartime, challenges come flying at Warriors from all angles and at all times. They can deal with this. They can flip from taking the big "helicopter" overall view to "fire-fighting" small but crucial issues.

They take what happens *personally*. They have to pull through and win, and they feel this need with every fiber of their being.

They take calculated *risks*. They leave as little as possible to chance, but they don't just let things drift along.

Warriors at all levels of the business have a sense of *dedication*. They go beyond the call of duty, acting for the greater good. They truly want to be part of something big.

"Wartime" periods represent some of the most challenging and dangerous moments in the life of an organization: during them, nothing is more important during than finding the right fit when it comes to people.

On the other hand, I have also encountered situations where the right fits are Peacetime CEO/executives.

These people keep things in *balance*: they keep things moving smoothly along 'in flow." They give the organization a "rhythm."

Peacetime CEOs are particularly good at *design and implementation*, putting the right policies, procedures, and processes in place at the right time.

At the same time, they are *aware*. They know fully well that threats may arise at any time. They hold an organization together and keep it well-organized so that if problems appear, they can be met.

They are very good at *scaling*, at taking organizations to the next level.

They stabilize and steady the ship, consolidate the gains, drive incremental and sustainable growth, and keep morale high.

Hiring Warrior CEO/executives and employees in peacetime would be disruptive and detrimental. The chances are high that if such a person were put in charge, the organization would start unnecessary "wars", e.g., initiating one restructuring initiative after another with no real justification for doing so other than probably boredom or the need to do something, anything. Fighting unnecessary battles and not picking one's fights carefully is the surest way an organization can set itself up to fail.

Another type of context is concerned with where the business is in its life cycle. As with "war" and "peace", the kind of people you need varies depending on this. The classic parts of the life cycle are:

1. Startup Phase

In this phase, you need people with pioneering spirits, an "insurgency mindset," lean orientation, and a drive for success. Employees must be required to work ungodly hours just for the business to stay afloat and to stand a chance of surviving and succeeding.

2. Growth Phase

In this phase, you need people who have "been there and done that." They must have the understanding and expertise to build scalable structures and systems.

3. Mature Phase

In this phase, you need experienced people who can stabilize, consolidate, and sustainably manage the business as well as innovate for a brighter future.

4. Turnaround Phase

Here you need people with track records and proven experience of successfully managing difficult situations, making extremely unpopular and tough choices, high levels of clarity and decisiveness, and an unmatched capacity to execute and manage complexity.

Irrespective of your current business context, I have outlined a "battle-tested" framework below: you can adapt and deploy it to ensure there is strong alignment between the realities of your business and your hiring decisions.

A Framework for Ensuring Contextualized Hiring

Step 1

Carry out an extensive diagnosis (as accurately as possible) to determine the internal and external realities that must be taken into due consideration when it comes to your staffing requirements. The sample questions in the model below will be hugely helpful in conducting effective context diagnostics.

Customer

- How are our customers' businesses/needs changing and how is this affecting our business?
- How are our customers' buying preferences and behavior changing and what are the implications for our company?
- What are the key frustrations clients encounter when using our various services/products?
- What are the unmet needs of our clients?
- Why do our current customers engage our services or use our products?
- What factors can potentially jeopardize our standing with our clients?
- What specific steps can we take to help clients who are buying our various services become more successful?
- Is there one thing across all our offerings that is difficult to do: but if we are able to accomplish, will blow our clients' mind? What is it?

Competition

- What is our definition of competitors? Is this definition serving us as well as we need it to serve us?
- What proactive steps are we taking to counter or decisively respond to our competitors' moves? What direct actions are we taking to confront competitive threats?

- What are our competitive advantages over our competitors? How do we leverage them for even greater advantages?
- Where are we at a disadvantage with respect to our competitors? What can we do to turn this around and gain competitive advantage?
- Where are we losing ground? How do we recover lost ground?
- Where are we gaining ground? How do we defend our position?
- In what ways can we extend our advantages to create more opportunities for us in the marketplace?

Company

- What are the obstacles standing in our way of achieving our strategic aspirations?
- What capabilities are essential to winning in our chosen areas of focus that are either lacking or inadequate? Which ones are lacking? Which ones are inadequate?
- What are our main weaknesses?
- What are our main strengths?
- What is one thing that is difficult to do but if we get it right will completely transform our business and enable us to achieve desired goals?
- Do we have the right people with the capabilities required to win in the market place?
- Are our best people working on our biggest opportunity?
- What activities MUST we prioritize and support with our best resources to increase our probability of success?
- What are the greatest opportunities we should be pursuing that have the greatest potential to accelerate our sustainable growth?

Market

- What are the key market considerations that we need to take into account when developing our business strategy?
- Where is the market/industry heading and what factors are shaping this journey?
- What are the opportunities and threats posed to our business by the happenings in the marketplace and how should we respond?

- What is the state of the economy and what impact are the related issues or concerns likely to have on our business?
- What is the state of our industry and how is this impacting on our business?

Step 2

Analyze the result of Step 1 to identify and document the most critical issues, broken down into two components, namely:

a. Problems/challenges that must be overcome to achieve the desired success with respect to the particular role for which you are hiring
b. Opportunities that must be created/captured to achieve the desired success with respect to that role

Step 3

Employ critical thinking to determine and articulate important implications of the business realities on the organization and the role your organization wants to hire for.

Step 4

Document your output from the exercise and use the resulting document (Success profile: Please refer to Chapter 3 for more on this) as a guide to help with hiring decision-making for the role.

CASE STUDY

How We Helped to Hire the Right COO

A few years ago, we received a brief from the Head of Human Resources (HHR) at a medium-sized organization (with about 150 employees) who was seeking our services to help the company hire a Chief Operating Officer (COO).

The job description we received from the HR department was rather too generic for our liking. Knowing from experience that our ability to successfully fill the role would be negatively affected if we didn't have the critical facts about the position, we requested to meet with the direct supervisor of the role—in this case, the CEO of the organization. We needed to "deep dive" and thoroughly understand the business context. But, our request was denied with the usual "The job description has all the information you need to fill the role successfully."

Having had similar experiences many times in the past, which usually resulted in a less than satisfactory outcome, we had a company policy that stopped us from taking on recruitment briefs for senior roles without engaging with the line manager or direct supervisor of the role.

We dug in and insisted that we would not be able to add value to the project without first discussing with the person who would be supervising and setting Key Performance Indicators (KPIs) for the role.

As luck would have it, this particular HHR was rational and reasonable. She said it would be difficult for her to arrange the meeting with the CEO because of his hectic schedule, but she would be more than willing to obtain a questionnaire from us that she could share with the CEO to get his input remotely.

Our preference, of course, was to engage directly with the

CEO so we could observe his body language, hear the tone of his voice, and feel the emotion while he discussed the brief and his particular needs.

However, we decided that engaging him via a questionnaire was better than non-engagement. We also believed that if he was the right type of CEO, there was a high likelihood of him granting us audience after going through our list of questions.

As it turned out, we were right. He was indeed an excellent CEO (one of the finest we have had the privilege of working with) and he requested a meeting with us the very next day to go over the diagnostic questions we had sent through his Head of Human Resources.

Needless to say, the meeting was extremely valuable to both parties. We, the consultants, had the opportunity to gain the insight and clarity needed to fill the role, and he was able to clarify the type of COO he needed to move his company forward.

From the diagnostic activities, we learned:

a. On the "3Cs + M" model, the company's Customers were being lured away by strong Competition. The general Market conditions were poor—the economy was not in a good state at that time. The Company had many issues, including poor customer service. It had experienced significant market share loss and a decline in revenue.

b. This period for the organization was definitely wartime.

c. Looking at the "four-phase" model, the company was in a serious turnaround situation.

d. The CEO was experiencing severe burnout and was completely overwhelmed with the demanding jobs of managing the complexity of a turnaround situation and running the business on a day-to-day basis.

e. The company needed to play two games of strategy effectively: the internal game of strategy (Operations,

People, Processes, Technology, Finance Management) without which they could not compete externally, and the external game of strategy (Sales, Relationship Management, Marketing, Client Services Management, Management of Regulators) without which they could not win and survive as a company.

f. The strength of the CEO lay in playing the external game of strategy. Hence, he needed a COO who was extremely capable and could play the internal game of strategy in line with the reality of the business.

g. To complement the role of the COO, the company also needed to set up a Project Management Office and hire a capable project manager to run and manage the turnaround activities.

h. Some of the top non-negotiables we identified for the COO role were the following:

- Strong finance background/orientation with excellent business acumen
- Prior work experience in a consulting/professional services firm
- Previous work experience as a COO in a turnaround situation
- Relevant prior industry experience
- Strong work ethic, ability to grind and follow-through (discipline of execution)
- The candidate needed to have an edge and to be decisive
- Excellent leadership skills

The information above formed the basis of the Success Profile we developed for the role (see Chapter 3 for more on Success Profiles) and the execution of the project.

The outcome was very successful as we were able to fill both the COO and the Project Manager roles. Thanks to these new employees, the company is now recovering lost ground and is back on a growth path once again. We would not have been able to achieve the desired result of identifying and hiring the right candidates for the roles without an in-depth understanding of the organizational context.

In Appendix 1 you can see a copy of the sample questionnaire we deployed during the role-diagnostic phase of our hiring-brief engagement, or you can visit **www.hiringrightbook.com** to download your free copy

KEY TAKEAWAYS

- When it comes to organizational success, context is everything. The degree of success will be determined by the degree of alignment of the company's activities with its internal and external realities.

- There are several ways of looking at contexts. One is to consider three external and one internal aspect. The three external ones are Customers, Market, and Competitors. The internal one is the nature and situation of the Company itself.

- Companies can be in "wartime" or "peacetime" situations. The kinds of people, especially leaders, needed at these different times are very different, and it can be a huge mistake to hire someone effective and skilled in one context when the company is in another one.

- Companies differ depending on what stages of growth they are in. The classic model differentiates between startups, growing companies, mature companies, and companies in stressed, "turnaround" situations.

- Prescription without diagnosis is malpractice. It is vital to conduct an extensive diagnosis of issues confronting the organization before determining its human capital requirements.

- As far as employee success in a role is concerned, "fit" is the main difference between right and wrong hiring decisions.

- A framework needs to be set up to ensure that all hiring decisions are taken in light of the current realities that the company is facing.

- Using generic job descriptions as the basis for making hiring decisions is illogical, dangerous, and doomed to failure. Organizations must stop doing this and adopt the best practices outlined in this chapter.

- The starting point of hiring right is confronting the realities of the organization, by understanding its context and identifying the human capital implications of that.

CHAPTER TWO

WITHOUT A CLEARLY DEFINED PROCESS, THE ODDS ARE STACKED AGAINST YOU

If you cannot describe what you are doing as a process, you don't know what you are doing."

Edward W Deming,

I often start my Hiring Training Workshop for Managers by asking each of them to draw a process flow chart of the hiring process they usually adopt when hiring on behalf of their organization.

I am yet to come across a company where one hundred percent of the managers respond to the challenge with the same process flow. In one extreme example, a group of fifteen managers from the same organization came up with fifteen different hiring process flow charts!

Organizations need to have standardized hiring processes that ensure consistency, predictability and quality of the hiring decision. Hiring right is way too important to leave to the discretion of hiring managers.

It's tough to imagine companies allowing their customer service representatives adopt whatever process or procedure they feel like when serving their customers. Doing so would be akin to allowing airline pilots fly aircraft any way they choose. Why, then, will organizations permit a situation where there are as many hiring processes as there are hiring managers within their organization?

I firmly believe that forward-looking organizations should do their utmost best to eliminate discretion at the operating levels of their business, and that this is particularly true for their hiring process. It's understandable and even acceptable for different organizations to have different recruitment processes, but it just shouldn't happen for an individual organization not to have a single hiring process that has the following characteristics:

- ✓ well thought through
- ✓ completely documented
- ✓ communicated to everyone
- ✓ agreed and used by all
- ✓ effectively enforced

I would love to be able to present a model process that everyone can use, to achieve this aim, at all times. However, years of helping numerous organizations develop their hiring processes have proven to me that the hiring process must be designed to fit the context and realities of the organization. One size does not fit all. The key to success is to develop a reliable process that works for your organization.

However, I hope the Case Study below will provide a model that can at least be used to inspire creativity in this essential area. It can be a benchmark for you to develop your own customized, purpose-fit and context-sensitive process.

CASE STUDY

How We Helped Our Client Create a Best-In-Class Hiring Process

One of our clients, a leading Telecommunication and Infrastructure Service Provider, approached us with a brief to help them develop a well-thought-through and scalable competency-based selection process and standard that they could adopt company-wide.

To execute this project, we deployed our road-tested methodology called the 5D process. The five D's are: Diagnose, Design, Develop, Deploy, and Drive.

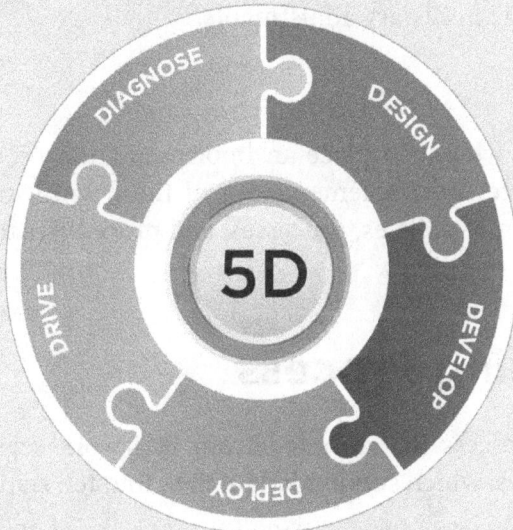

Diagnose

We started by identifying where they currently were with respect to their hiring process. We benchmarked the organization's hiring process against best practices. Then we identified and documented the gaps.

Design

Based on the identified gaps, we co-designed a high-level hiring process and validated it with key stakeholders.

Develop

We took the approved high-level hiring process and from it developed the various components and relevant instruments to drive the process.

Deploy

Then we organized a pilot project to test the new process with stakeholders, learnt all the lessons, course-corrected, and made the necessary adjustments.

Drive

Finally, we put in place an implementation process to drive the successful implementation of the new hiring process in the form of policies, processes, and procedures to achieve the desired objectives.

The Hiring Process

The hiring process that resulted from this work segmented into three distinct phases, which subdivided further, into ten steps. The phases were:

- **The Preparation Phase** – What must happen before engagement with candidates

- **The Assessment Phase** – What must happen during candidate engagement
- **The Follow up Phase** – What needs to happen after candidate engagement

Preparation Phase

The preparation phase is made up of four distinct steps:

Step 1: Conduct a competent Job Analysis (see a full Job Analysis template and download at **www.hiringbook.com**).

Step 2: Develop accurate Job Descriptions (see a full Job Description template and download at **www.hiringrightbook.com**).

Step 3: Engage and consult with subject matter/job expert/line managers to:

a) Identify the most critical job tasks and deliverables

b) Determine non-negotiable competencies that predict exceptional performance on the job

Step 4: Develop relevant behavioral-based interview questions and assessment instruments (visit and download sample behavioral-based questions/assessment instruments at **www.hiringrightbook.com**).

Assessment Phase

This phase is made up of three distinct steps:

Step 5: Welcome the candidates and explain the details of the job and the selection process.

Step 6: Conduct the selection process by asking agreed questions, deploying agreed instruments, and ensuring proper capture of relevant information.

Step 7: Close the selection process, thank the candidates, and give them information regarding the next stage(s) in the hiring process.

Follow-up Phase

Step 8: Carry out critical review/scoring of candidate's performance against set standards.

Step 9: Make a selection decision based on this.

Step 10: Communicate the outcome to candidates.

Hiring Right Process Diagram

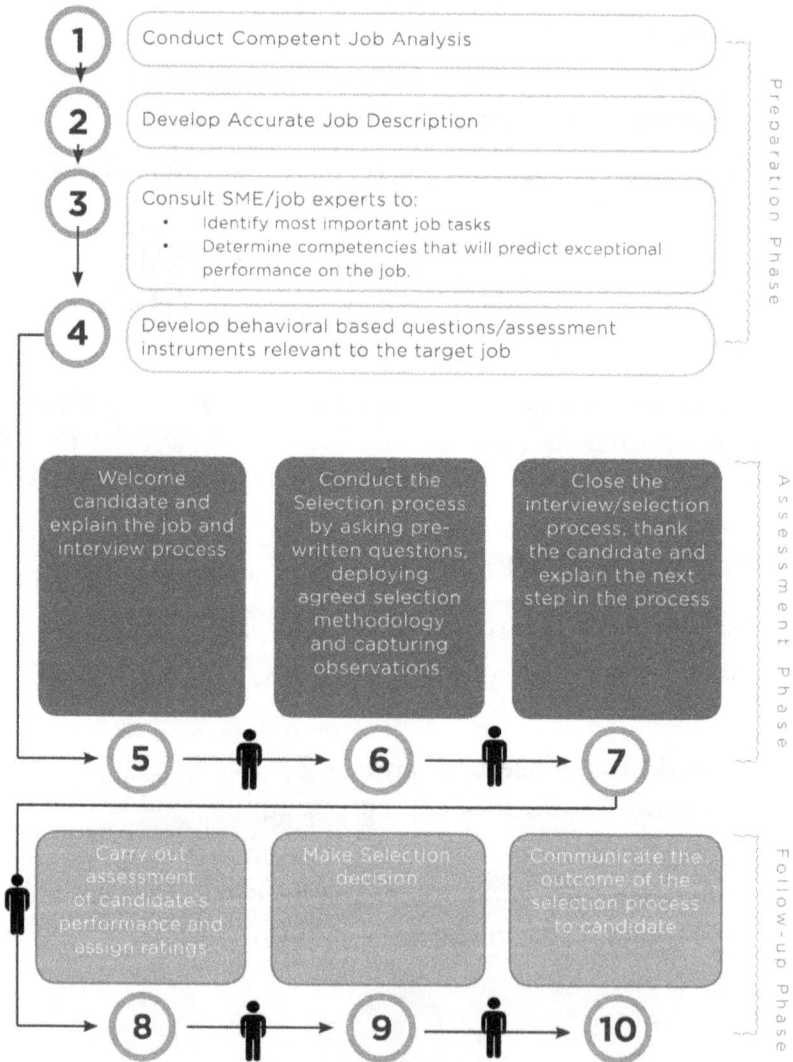

Once we were done creating the hiring process, we trained selected hiring managers & HR professionals in the company on the methodology (please refer to Chapter 4 for more on this).

With a well-defined, standardized Hiring process in place, adopted by all hiring managers, the company experienced significant increase in the quality of people being hired into the organization.

Your company can experience similar improvement in the quality of your new hires, if you invest in creating a well-thought-through, properly documented, company-wide adopted and enforced hiring standards.

KEY TAKEAWAYS

- To build a world-class organization, you must develop and implement a world-class hiring process.
- Organizations must do whatever it takes to eliminate randomness in their hiring process. They must recognize this simple truth: No standards, no sustainable success.
- If you're hiring for one organization or one brand, a uniform process is essential to a successful outcome.
- Our ten-step model is an excellent one that can be modeled after...
- ...But every organization should tailor it to their specific contexts and realities.

CHAPTER THREE

SUCCESS LEAVES CLUES

"You can teach a turkey to climb a tree, but I'd rather hire a squirrel."

Lyle Spencer

One of the most critical questions organizations must ask and answer before embarking on any initiative is, "By the time we are done, what will success look like?" Sadly, most organizations fail to ask and answer this question clearly, and this is one of the major root causes of failure in organizations.

When it comes to hiring right, before you do anything else, you must ask the question, "What will success look like for the target role?" This needs to be answered in terms of who the ideal person should be and what levels of performance and contribution are required of the person. This is absolutely non-negotiable if your organization is going to achieve its desired goals and objectives.

The answer to this question is the Success Profile.

A Success Profile serves as a standard against which we can measure potential candidates for a particular role. Without it, recruitment exercises will be like a situation where a hunter goes into the forest and fires his arrow indiscriminately with the hope that a deer will run into one. When it comes to hiring right, hope is not a good enough strategy. Hiring the right people is a matter of life and death and it's way too important to leave to chance.

Success profiling is based on two profoundly simple but extremely powerful concepts:

1. **Success leaves clues** – if we can identify what created success in the first place and can replicate these conditions, we stand a high chance of recreating that success.

2. **Begin with the end in mind** – if we can make an effort to think through and determine what success should look like at the end of the intervention, our likelihood of achieving a successful outcome increases significantly.

CASE STUDY

How Scientists Used Success Profiling to Eliminate a Horrible Disease Without Finding a Cure

Thirty years ago, more than 2.25 million people in 22,000 villages were suffering from the horrific disease known as Guinea Worm. This caused devastation for the infected individual and for their family. If parents were infected, their livelihood was jeopardized, whether it was fishing, farming or something else.

Thank goodness, social scientists were able to reduce the incidence of this horrible disease. Such was the efficacy of their approach that there were fewer than twenty-two reported cases globally by 2014. Even more remarkable is the fact that they didn't find any cure or vaccine for the disease (although it's known to be caused by the parasitic worm *Dracunculus medinensis*). So how did they achieve this? And most importantly, what lessons can businesses learn from their feat that can significantly increase our probability of successfully hiring the right people?

The social scientists searched for and identified villages with similar profiles/demography to the ones that had been devastated with the disease but were not affected by it. They studied the villagers' actions and behaviors to learn the specific things that they did differently (the differentiating factors).

They identified three vital (differentiating) behaviors:

1. In unaffected villages, people always filtered their water before consumption. Sometimes the village women made use of crude methods for this purpose, including the usage of the clothes they wore as the water filter.

2. Once an individual contracted the disease, the person was

isolated from the village's water source to prevent further spreading of the dreaded disease—eggs from the wound of the infected person would be released if the person came in contact with the water thereby causing further pollution and infection.

3. If the villagers discovered anyone not filtering their water, they would use social pressure to isolate and compel the guilty to comply. The individual wouldn't be allowed to attend village meetings or participate in traditional rites or celebrations like the New Yam festival.

These three vital behaviors were then taught in the villages in which the disease was endemic. The result was phenomenal. This approach to studying successful communities, learning their critical, differentiating behaviors, codifying it, and using that knowledge to help other communities in trouble accounted for the eradication of Guinea Worm disease.

Businesses can take a cue from how a horrible disease like Guinea Worm was eradicated without ever finding a cure to improve their hiring process.

What is a Success Profile?

"In determining the right people, the good-to-great companies placed greater weight on character attributes than on specific educational background, practical skills, specialized knowledge, or work experience."

Jim Collins

To explain the concept of a Success Profile, I would like you to carry out this exercise.

Close your eyes and picture someone you know who is very successful in their field of endeavor—in fact, so successful that you admire and would want to emulate this person or make them your role model. It doesn't matter what the field of endeavor is: business, sport, religion, and music…

whatever area you can think of.

Now open your eyes.

Take a piece of paper and draw a line vertically down the middle to divide it into two halves.

Draw a horizontal line to divide one of the halves into two halves.

Label the three boxes that this creates A, B, and C.

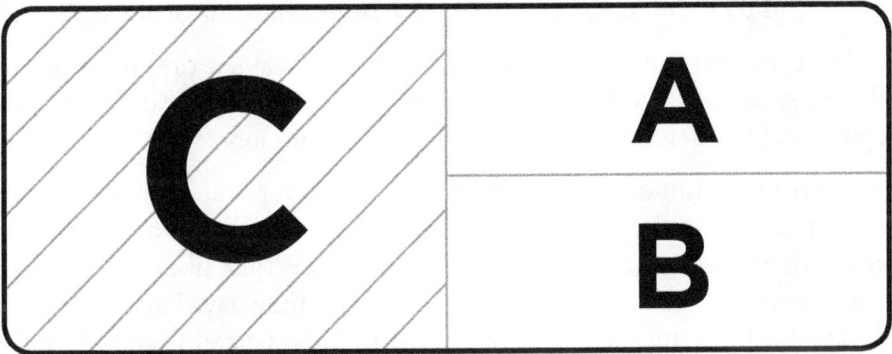

I can tell you the secret to the success of your selected role model based on the exercise above:

- *Sector A* represents their *skill*, which is defined as the learned ability to do something really well. The individual(s) you selected are highly skilled in their chosen field of endeavor.
- *Sector B* represents *knowledge*, which is the body of relevant information possessed in a given area. Your role model has an in-depth understanding of their chosen field.
- *Sector C* represents the *characteristics* that they exhibit, which predict or inform their success. These characteristics are sometimes referred to as attitude or model of behavior.

You will notice that the most significant section is that of the characteristics. It is the size of the other two combined, which is a measure of its relative importance to success in business and life in general.

The combination of the knowledge, skills, and characteristics required for success or superior performance in a particular role or area of endeavor is the Success Profile.

In the thought experiment above, you modeled someone you admire.

But the method can be used for any role. Who fulfills the role excellently, and what do they do?

Study your best performers.

Top performers tend not to stick exactly to job descriptions. Instead, as they learn exactly what it takes to do their job really well, the best employees expand their activities beyond the boundaries of the basic job description they were handed at the beginning. They do new things or old things slightly differently. They learn new skills. They make new contacts.

For the organization as a whole to make the best use of this creativity, what they do well and how they do it need to be captured, so they can be replicated by other, less effective holders of similar jobs.

Even more important, the learning can be replicated so that if the creative employee decides to leave—which they may do—it can be passed on to others. Sadly, people outgrow organizations (just like organizations outgrow some of their people). If you wait until they have handed in their notice, it will be too late to really capture the essence of what they do. Success Profiling needs to be an ongoing process, a continual examination of what your best people are doing and what exactly that entails.

CASE STUDY

The Danger of Not Studying Top Performers

Use reverse engineering by discovering what the very best know, do and how they think and leverage the data to improve hiring success".

George Anders

Angie was a superb medical receptionist. She kept records accurately, had first-rate typing and shorthand skills, could read the doctors' handwriting very well, and was always punctual. She was a people person and possessed exceptional interpersonal skills. All the customers loved Angie dearly because of her ability to make them forget why they were visiting the hospital.

When she resigned, an advertisement was placed and a new receptionist, Jumai, was hired. However, she was a disaster. Although she performed all the most obvious duties of a receptionist adequately, the surgery became an unhappy place: patients complained, waiting time increased, and the business started to lose money.

What went wrong? What was responsible for this problem? What do you think was the principal element of Angie's job that was not being performed by Jumai?

A thorough analysis of Angie's duties would have revealed that patient/customer care and interpersonal relationship competence were vital components of the job. Failure to identify this was the primary cause of the recruitment error. Modeling Angie in respect of the job function would have allowed us to identify key characteristics and behavioral competencies that made her a superior performer.

This information could then have been used to create a Success Profile that would have ensured that only those candidates who were able to demonstrate competencies identified as critical to successful performance on the job would be considered as Angie's replacement.

Studying Top Performers

So, how do you study Top Performers to identify what makes them tick? You can deploy various methodologies:

Job Analysis Interviews

- The interview starts with a question about the four or five most critical primary responsibilities in the job.
- When these have been identified, the interviewer focuses on each

primary responsibility and asks about:

- ♦ Key tasks for this responsibility
- ♦ Skills and knowledge required to perform the functions for this primary responsibility
- ♦ The performance criteria or measures used to assess performance in the job
- The information gathered will then be documented appropriately in a Job Profile to be used as part of the guide for hiring new employees into the role.

Resource Panels

- A resource panel is a three-to-six–hour facilitated meeting with an agenda that is similar to but broader than the one covered in a Job Analysis Interview. The participants usually include three to four capable job incumbents, three to four managers of job incumbents, and one to two HR staff who work closely with job incumbents or at least have an understanding of what they do.
- A resource panel has three main purposes:
  - ♦ To gather data needed to identify the competencies for the job.
  - ♦ To build consensus among a set of key stakeholders about what the job requires and
  - ♦ To build support for the study project

Behavioral Event Interviews

- A Behavioral Event Interview is a one-hour interview in which the interviewee is asked to provide highly detailed accounts of how they approached four-to-seven important accomplishments or other critical events from the past year or two in the job. The interviewer uses a probing strategy to get the interviewee to walk through the sequence of what they did, said, and thought at crucial points during each accomplishment or event.
- The assumption underlying the interview is that studying the interviewee's actions, thoughts, and words in these critical situations will reveal the underlying competencies responsible for superior performance.

- This process can be taken further and deeper through a Key Event Interview, with the subject identifying *one* particular time when they did something extraordinarily well, and being asked to look deeply into what they did, said, and thought during that process.

Direct Observation of Incumbent

- Direct observation of incumbents on the job offers a reality check against the information gathered during interviews. Spending a full day with someone and observing what the person does enables you to weed out idealized reports and create a more realistic picture of effective job behaviors.
- One potential problem with the direct observation method of study is that the mere presence of an observer changes the environment and behavior of the person being observed; therefore, the observer should be as unobtrusive as possible.

Please visit **www.hiringrightbook.com** to download detailed templates for conducting effective Job Analysis Interviews, Resource Panel Sessions, Behavioral Event Interviews, and Direct Observations.

CASE STUDY

Developing Success Profiles For A Critical Role

"I noticed that the dynamic range between what an average person could accomplish and what the best person could accomplish was 50 or 100 to 1. Given that, you're well advised to go after the cream of the cream. A small team of A+ players can run circles around a giant team of B and C players."

Steve Jobs

Our firm recently won a project to assist a high-growth company in the Financial Services sector with its Business Improvement and Growth Advisory project. As part of the project, we were required to co-create with them their three-year strategic plan and design a context-relevant Strategic Workforce Plan (SWP) that would enable the company to execute its strategy and achieve their desired goals and objectives.

During the design and development phase of the project, we identified the company's mission-critical role (the role without which they would not successfully execute their strategy) as that of the strategic account manager.

Further analysis of the context of the role and assessment of the incumbent capabilities and bench strength revealed two alarming and potentially disastrous issues waiting to happen:

1   We identified huge performance variation between the very best, the good, and the average Key Account Managers across the organization. To make matters worse, the best Key Account Managers were in the minority by a high margin—less than three percent of the total workforce performing the critical role.

Figure 2-1: Performance Curve showing how performance is distributed across an organization.

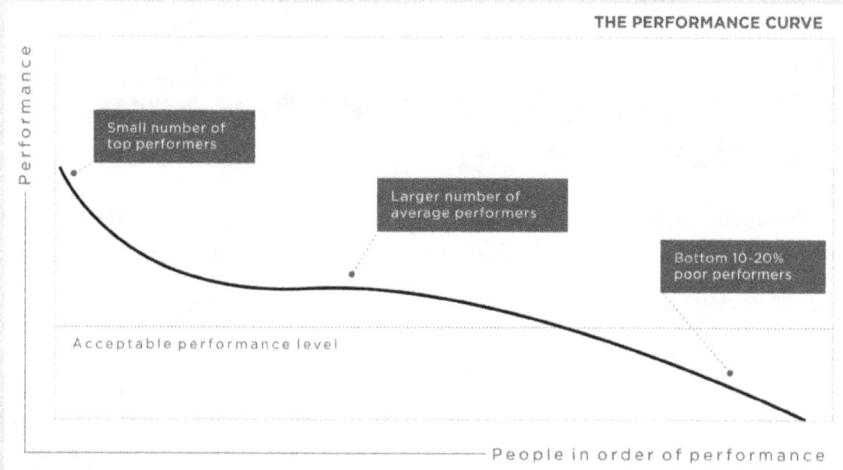

THE PERFORMANCE CURVE

Performance

Small number of
top performers

Larger number of
average performers

Bottom 10-20%
poor performers

Acceptable performance level

People in order of performance

2   A Stay Interview Survey revealed that about sixty-five percent of the top producing Account Managers were a

flight risk (meaning there was a high chance of them leaving the company), which could potentially have dramatic impacts on the business of the organization (Go to Appendix 2 to view a copy of Stay Interview or log on to **www.hiringrightbook.com** to download a Stay Interview template for your use).

We presented our report to the project committee, and they immediately grasped the implication of our report and the need to urgently address the problem.

The solutions we proffered to the organization are as follows:

1. Do everything possible to retain the top-performing Key Account Managers

2. Accelerate the development of the good/average Key Account Managers

3. Hire better Key Account Managers to replace the perennial below-average ones

In this study, I'll concentrate on our solutions to issues 2 and 3. I will talk more about the very important issue of retention of top people in Chapter 9.

To successfully implement 2 and 3 above, the starting point was to carry out an extensive study of the top-performing Key Account Managers and identify what they did differently: the differentiating skills, knowledge, and characteristics that were predictors of their superior performance. In other words, the Success Profile for the job. The Profile was essential in the design and development of a pragmatic, targeted application-focused curriculum for the development of the good/average Key Account Managers.

We deployed the following tools/methodologies/approaches to carry out the study of the Top Performers.

a. Behavioral Event Interviews with the individual Top Performer and their line manager.

b. Direct Observations, which involved attending client

engagement meetings and spending time to observe "A Day in Life" (see Chapter 6) of the Key Account Managers.

Going through the process above enabled us to identify the key differentiating factor between the best Key Account Managers and the rest:

- They had a deep understanding of their customers' specific business contexts
- They had a strong grasp of business and used this to educate their customers, sharing research and ideas
- They had excellent product knowledge
- They were consummate professionals, always smart, respectful, and on time
- They really cared about their customers' success
- They asked the right questions to uncover customer needs, like a doctor diagnosing an illness

The information we gathered and codified was then used to develop a custom program that included role-play, simulations, projects, and assessments for the development of the average Account Managers.

The same information was developed into an induction program that was used to onboard the new hires. Within twelve months of deployment, the performance of the organization, with respect to its key account management metrics, improved by seven percent, mostly due to the improvement and contribution of the well-trained existing team and the newly hired Key Account Managers

"If you can hire people whose passion intersects with the job, they won't require any supervision at all. They will manage themselves better than anyone could ever manage them. Their fire comes from within, not from without. Their motivation is internal, not external."

Stephen Covey

KEY TAKEAWAYS

- Most organizations have staff performing at very different levels.
- Do whatever it takes to find out what differentiates successful people in your organizations (your Top Performers) from the rest.
- Use the information to create Success Profiles.
- These are essential recruitment tools, but can also be used to raise the performance bar across the organization.
- Identify and study your Top Performers while they are embedded in and committed to the organization. If you leave this process till after they have decided to leave, you will not be modeling best practice.
- A simple Success Profile looks at skill, knowledge, and characteristics of the incumbent in a particular role.
- Of these, characteristics is the most important.
- There are a number of ways of creating such Profiles. These include job analysis interviews, resource panels, behavioral event interviews, and direct observation.

CHAPTER FOUR

"I WOULDN'T DO THAT IF I WERE YOU" - THE DANGERS OF ALLOWING UNTRAINED MANAGERS MAKE HIRING DECISIONS

"There is nothing training cannot do. Nothing is above its reach. It can turn bad morals into good ones; it can destroy bad principles and recreate good ones; it can lift men and women to angelship."

Mark Twain

When we begin a Hiring Managers Capability Development project with clients, we conduct a poll among the students to find out if they have had previous formal training on how to hire right. Usually less than a quarter of the hands in the room go up.

When we ask a follow-up question regarding whether they have ever gone through a formal Hiring Practices Certification program, we mostly get just one or two hands going up. Not coincidentally these individuals always have two things in common: they have previously worked in a world-class or global organization, and they agree that the skill to hire right is one of the most valuable ones they possess.

From our experience, most organizations don't believe it is imperative to train and certify their hiring managers on their company's standardized hiring process. Instead, they assume that their managers are competent when it comes to effective recruitment. This is a perilous assumption.

We have also encountered managers who believe attending a program on how to hire right is a waste of their time. We typically hear comments like, "Look, I've been hiring for the past ten, fifteen, twenty, twenty-five years and I know all I need to know."

However, when we dig deeper, we typically discover that most of these "experienced managers" have been "winging it" when it comes to hiring and don't follow any well-defined or consistent process when hiring. No consistency, no predictable result—it's that simple.

The health of a business is not significantly different from that of human beings. An ounce of prevention is worth a pound of cure. And when it comes to the well-being of a company, doing whatever it takes to prevent the deadly disease of wrong hiring starts with ensuring your hiring managers are well trained in the practice of hiring the right people. This is probably the most essential skill required of managers in the current business climate.

Yet I am constantly amazed at the sheer number of organizations I've come across that have never bothered to train their managers on how to do this. Can you imagine airlines not training their pilots on how to land a plane safely or doctors not being shown how to effectively diagnose their patient's disease? All the other know-how they possess will have little usefulness without this critical knowledge. And the same applies to your hiring managers.

Best-in-class organizations certify their hiring managers on the company's standard recruitment process and methodologies. And just as pilots and doctors are required to be recertified to keep current and up-to-date with their crafts, designated hiring managers should go through a hiring recertification process every three to four years.

Best practices in hiring the right employees should be mandatory training for hiring managers in every organization.

Creating an Effective Hiring Training Program

All employees involved in the hiring process must be trained in and certified on their organization's hiring practices and processes. The program should be designed with an application focus, i.e., with lots of opportunities for practice. It should be highly practical with a minimal amount of theory.

Many training programs make the mistake of blitzing the delegates with loads of information but giving them little or no time for practice. The participants leave the programs with a healthy glow, which they maintain for a few days after the event. Then they go back to the old ways of doing things.

Usually, the assumption is that when you receive a lot of information from a training program, you've received a lot of value. This assumption is faulty for two main reasons:

1) Nobody gets good at anything without loads of practice and repetition. Information does not create competence, only application does.

2) The greatest gap in both life and business is the gap between knowing and doing. The fact that you know doesn't mean that you will do what you know. However, with loads of practice, your probability of applying what you know and putting in an excellent performance increases efficiently.

If each of us hires people who are smaller than we are, we shall become a company of dwarfs. But if each of us hires people who are bigger than we are, we shall become a company of giants"

David Ogilvy

Our own training curriculum for hiring practices is designed with a focus on application. We incorporate videos, role-plays, peer interviews, and live interview sessions. Delegates get to practice their newly acquired skills multiple times with real candidates under close observation and receive real-time feedback on how they can improve.

The experiential learning nature of the program makes it extremely valuable for delegates, as they get to apply what they have learned and perfect their skills before they complete the workshop. Visit **www. hiringrightbook.com** to download a copy of our general hiring practices curriculum.

What makes a great hirer?

Naturally, my first response to this is that they've been properly trained! However, it's worth looking at the other traits of people who excel in this role.

As well as knowing the structures and processes, they *value* and respect them, and understand at a deep level how important these are. Poor hirers know the structures and processes, but in their hearts think that these things are there to assist their own personal intuition and can be got round whenever necessary.

Great hirers are *committed* to the task. They know how important their role is. So they will put all their effort into finding the right person and will do whatever it takes to make this happen.

Great hirers are deep *listeners*. In turn, good listeners practice a number of crucial habits — I have put them in the opposite box.

BEING A GOOD LISTENER

Create rapport with the interviewee

Don't try and face them down or make them feel small. Establish eye contact.

Keep this rapport during the conversation, nodding from time to time or interjecting little phrases like "I see" or even just "Uh-huh."

Attend to the interviewee

Make sure you aren't distracted by background noise or any mannerisms of the speaker. It is their words and their emotional reactions that matter.

Quiet your own internal voices

Poor listeners only half attend to others. The other half of their concentration is on themselves, what question they're going to ask next, "How the interview is going", and so on.

Stay on message

It's very easy to get led down a conversational dead-end. "Oh, so you come from such-and-such town. I've been there..." A little bit of this can create rapport but beware of doing too much of this. It moves the focus of the conversation onto you and your experiences, whereas the focus needs to be on the applicant.

Make sure the interviewee doesn't do this to you as well!

Ask open questions

Make sure your questions invite the other person to expand on what they've just said, as opposed to closed questions which only invite a yes or no answer.

Open questions are introduced with interrogatives like how, what, where, when, why and who.

Ask for clarification whenever you need it

Self-evident—but many people don't do it often out of a fear that they will look stupid at not having understood the other person. Ask for clarification as soon as you feel you are losing the thread of what the other person is saying, the good listener waits for an appropriate pause—you shouldn't just interrupt people mid-sentence—and then ask for clarification. Having asked, make sure you're back on track.

Summarize from time to time

Check you are on track with questions like: "So you didn't feel satisfied at XYZ company because there was too much micro-management, am I right?"

Watch as well as listen

People can convey a huge amount of information via non-verbal clues clues (physical body movements, facial expressions, nuances in their voice tone). If someone says they care deeply about something and look genuinely engaged, then they probably do.

Sadly, this can also be information to the effect that they are lying, or at least embroidering the truth.

Above all, perhaps, good listening is about a mindset. It's about genuinely wanting to know about the other person.

Good hirers are *courteous* and pleasant. This doesn't mean weak; they know what they want and make sure they get it.

They are *thorough*. They take time to prepare before the interview. I have known many managers who do no preparation before an interview.

A candidate arrives. The manager says, "What's your name?" and begins leafing through a pile of CVs, finally finding the right one. This is an appalling practice.

Good hirers *prepare* long before the interview.

They will do their "due diligence" of the role. They will consider what the role is and why it is important. How does it fit the organization? They will look at how performance of the role will be measured. What will the KPIs be? They will study (or create) the Success Profile for the role.

Based on this, they will work out the best questions to ask and write these down in sequence. Many good hirers add positive and negative indicators for each question.

They will also study the applicants' CVs. They make notes on each one. Are there gaps? Are there areas where they want to dig deeper?

This work will be kept in a proper file, along with the applicants CVs. This may sound obvious, but I have seen managers carry out interviews with relevant papers strewn all over their desks.

They leave time before the interview—a quarter of an hour is ideal. They take out the questions and run through them so that when they ask them, they sound natural. Most important, they reread the applicant's CV and revisit the notes they made on it.

Hiring right takes time. I shall say more on this later.

"First-rate people hire first-rate people; second-rate people hire third-rate people."

Leo Rosten

KEY TAKEAWAYS

- Companies must train and certify their hiring managers. The benefits of doing so far outweigh the cost. Not training your hiring managers is a big mistake.

- The training must be designed with a focus on application. It must include lots of practice and repetition. Information doesn't create competence. Application does.

- The creation of hiring standards and processes must precede the training so that what the participants are learning to apply are the standards that have been designed and validated as being adequate for ensuring the right people are hired.

- Hiring is a complex skill. It involves specific abilities, such as proper listening and the ability to ask the right kind of questions, with a mindset that is committed to the process, understands its importance, and is respectful of the candidate.

- Hiring takes time. Too many managers hire "on the hoof," leafing through piles of CVs as candidates arrive in the room. To hire well, you must think carefully about the role to be filled and study each candidate's CV before you meet them.

CHAPTER FIVE

MIND THE GAP – HOW PERSONAL BIAS LEADS TO POOR HIRING DECISIONS

"Human beings are poor examiners, subject to superstition, bias, prejudice, and a PROFOUND tendency to see what they want to see rather than what is really there."

M. Scott Peck

Bias in candidate selection decision-making is a major reason why organizations fail to hire right. No matter how intelligent, knowledgeable, and experienced you are in hiring—even if you're an authority on the subject and have written a book—you're still very much susceptible to making a wrong hiring decision as a result of your biases.

Based on a careful analysis of hiring mistakes that I've personally made in the past twenty years (and those of others that I am intimately aware of), I have come to the conclusion that everyone has a "Bias Code" that can be activated positively or negatively during a hiring process and that can potentially lead to undesirable outcomes. This code consists of psychological triggers specific to the individual.

Once a candidate unlocks one or two of these triggers, the interview is essentially over. The triggers are so powerful that once they are activated, all reasoning flies out of the window. The activated code takes over completely and dominates proceedings from that point on. No matter how compelling the contrary evidence is, once the "code" takes hold, it is essentially game over.

My Bias Code can be triggered by what a candidate says or writes, the way they appear or behave, and their level of confidence (or lack of it).

What are your Bias Code triggers? Do trust me when I say that you have some and that you will benefit significantly from acknowledging this fact (you are only human after all), from doing everything humanly possible to identify them, and then from developing practical approaches and mental models to ensure that your Bias Code doesn't get activated and unconsciously trip you up when making hiring decisions.

Don't think that you're uniquely above such things. You are not. You may well be a person with no prejudices based on the major factors that divide humanity: race, class, nationality, education level, gender, and faith. But bias can still creep in.

As well as individual biases, there are biases built into our basic, shared human psychology. The notion of the "confirmation bias" described below has been around since the dawn of history. The ancient Greek historian Thucydides described it, and it was also discussed by medieval European philosophers. Modern scientific research on the topic began in the 1960s, and it is now a well-understood phenomenon.

Here are some typical bias triggers.

Trigger 1: First Impression

Many hiring managers draw conclusions about their candidates very quickly—sometimes as quickly as within thirty seconds of meeting them. These can then sway how you conduct the rest of the interview. You might end up asking easier questions if you had a positive first impression, or more difficult questions if it was negative. First impressions can set the stage for a domino effect of other biases.

Trigger 2: Confirmation Bias

Confirmation bias is sometimes the by-product of first impressions, while at other times it is a symptom of feeling pressured to hire someone quickly.

Have you ever watched a courtroom drama where the prosecutor is interrogating the defendant, and the defendant's lawyer leaps to their feet and says, "Objection! Leading the witness!" and the judge says, "Sustained!" Confirmation bias is just like that, except there's no judge in the room to point out your faulty conduct when you're asking the wrong questions in an interview.

In other words, you're asking the candidate irrelevant or very pointed questions to get the response that supports what you already decided about them thirty seconds after they entered the room.

When looking for an editor for this book, I received a reply from someone whose tone really appealed to me. She said she had "years of experience," and I was so impressed by her that I never asked to see samples of books she had edited. When I asked if she had carried out a project like mine before, she responded affirmatively. Because that was what I wanted to hear already, I took that as sufficient confirmation. But the end result of the engagement told a different story and I had to hire another editor.

Trigger 3: The "Halos and Horns" Effect

One detail or fact about the candidate can result in your thinking that they're either a heaven-sent angel or a demon intending to burn your business to the ground. In the example of my interview with the editor, she told a story about a CEO she had previously worked with who had almost failed due to poor strategy—until she (the editor) entered the picture.

That was when my "halo" bias trigger was activated. From then on, I saw her as a figure with almost magical powers, and nothing else she said or did could have dispelled the notion that this was the editor I'd been looking for.

There's a flip side to this bias, called the "horns" effect, which is when you zero in on a factor that you consider negative and harmful. After the activation of this bias, there's nothing the candidate can do to redeem themselves in your mind.

For example, you find out that an applicant doesn't have a university degree and you decide they're not educated enough for the job, regardless of how much in-field experience or skill they have.

Trigger 4: Similarity and Affinity

It's only human to be drawn to things that are familiar or relatable. If you discover a commonality with your candidate, be aware of the fact that you may be swayed to favor them over other candidates. For example, if they went to the same university as you, or you're both really into sports (or worse still, you support the same team). The more the candidate reminds you of yourself, the more likely you are to feel they are the best candidate for the job.

Ironically, the truth is often the opposite: it is diversity in skills, strengths, and other characteristics that will help your business grow so it can often be valuable to hire someone that you don't have too much in common with.

Trigger 5: Jumping to Conclusions

The scientific term for this is the "affect heuristic," which means the tendency to make quick judgments about a person, usually based on your personal or emotional response. Such subconcious occurences play a part in nearly every decision we make.

You might already see how this could cause issues when it comes to interviewing potential recruits. For example, if you're conducting an interview with someone who reminds you of a horrible boss/colleague you once had, you might pass them over despite their qualifications due to the negative feelings that resurface.

However, it can be far subtler than that. Even the way a candidate smiles can trigger an evolutionary response that you interpret as being either sincere or insincere.

Trigger 6: Turning a Blind Eye to Red Flags

Sometimes called the "ostrich effect," this bias is when you ignore a major red flag because so much else about the candidate seems to be a good fit.

Red flags can be sent out when a confident candidate begins to shade into arrogance. To return to my editor story, at one point, this person said that they charged a high fee because "blockheads" charged less. Labeling fellow editors in this way was deeply unprofessional and should have been a bright red flag. I overlooked it easily because everything else the person wrote was telling me exactly what I wanted to hear.

Trigger 7: Appearance Bias

We subconsciously judge people's capabilities based on what they look like. For example, one study found that CEOs tend to be taller than the average person. This is because we subconsciously see someone who is tall as being someone we can look up to (in both the literal and figurative sense).

Perceived beauty also wreaks havoc on our judgment. People who are "generally attractive" are often subconsciously perceived as more persuasive and capable. Yet, women who are considered "extremely attractive" are actually less likely to be hired. They are often erroneously perceived as less competent and authoritative than their more "average-looking" counterparts.

Trigger 8: Bandwagon effect (Groupthink)

The term Groupthink, first used by George Orwell in his novel *1984* was promoted as a serious psychological term by William H. Whyte in 1952, to describe the way people in groups tend to converge in their opinions. Subsequent research, especially by Professor Irving Janis of Yale University, refined the concept. Janis pointed out that there was an irony to this: the more cohesive and energetic a group was (a good thing), the more susceptible it was to this phenomenon, which can be disastrous.

Groupthink is particularly common if the group has a powerful leader: the opinions of the group will converge around that person's views—or around what people think the views of the leader are. If the leader is not clear, a deeply confusing situation can arise when people think the leader thinks "x" and act accordingly, while actually, the leader thinks "y" but hasn't expressed themselves very well.

In hiring, this can be a serious problem if a panel is interviewing the candidate, especially where one panel member is more senior or a persuasive, charismatic "alpha."

Trigger 9: The Bias Blind Spot

Sadly, most of us have a secret belief that while other people are biased, we have risen above such weakness and have mastered the art of objectivity. This is part of a bigger phenomenon whereby we tend to overrate our own skills relative to those of other people.

This is known as the Dunning-Kruger effect, named after two social psychologists, David Dunning and Justin Kruger. This is a cognitive bias in which people overrate their own abilities.

Interestingly, Dunning and Kruger argued that "the miscalibration of the incompetent stems from an error about the self, whereas the miscalibration of the highly competent stems from an error about others." In other words, people of low ability misjudge themselves, and people of high ability misjudge the world out there. Either way, we are incapable of accurately assessing our own capabilities.

In an experiment carried out at Stanford University in 2002, ninety-one students were rated on their ability to pass a set of tests. They were then asked to assess their own performance (without seeing the actual results). Seventy-nine of them (eighty-seven percent) rated themselves as "better than average."

Subsequent experiments have confirmed this phenomenon around the world.

Trigger 10: Overconfidence

The bias blind spot becomes worse when we're doing something we've done before—even if we've done it badly. I often hear managers say, "I've been doing this a long time; I know a talent when I see one!"

It's this line of thinking that leads to the worst kind of hiring mistakes. Like an experienced driver who has never been in an accident before, it desensitizes you to the possible dangers, and that's when you let your guard down and make a mistake. This goes to show you that hiring bias can affect *even the most seasoned recruiters* because they may feel they have a knack for selecting the right candidate and put more stock in their "gut instincts."

How to Rise Above Your Hiring Bias

"Fortunately for serious minds, a bias recognized is a bias sterilized."

Benjamin Haydon

It's easy to see how these hiring biases can have devastating effects on your business. So what's a hiring manager to do? We can't help but be human, but that doesn't mean there aren't ways to stay actively objective during the hiring process. Keeping to the best practices below can help you make smarter decisions:

Follow a Uniform and Proven Process – Uniform conduct will help you stay objective by committing to run each candidate through an identical process, regardless of what your impressions or feelings are. Create a Standard Operating Procedure for yourself and other hiring staff to stay on track from the time you start looking at résumés to the time you send out the job offer.

Don't Rush a Decision – Never hire someone directly after interviewing them. Even if you needed someone to start yesterday, hiring the wrong person can have more severe consequences than muddling through until you're able to find the best person for the job.

Examine the Red Flags – Red flags can be easy to overlook when you're eager to hire someone. To be sure, a red flag doesn't necessarily or always mean that the candidate is a wrong fit. However, if you spot such a flag, you will need to dig deeper to get a better understanding of who you're hiring. For example, if a candidate shows up late for their interview, that's a red flag. Instead of overlooking it, ask the candidate why it happened and pay close attention to their response and demeanor.

Do Preliminary Interviews by Phone or Email – You can reduce some of your susceptibility to appearance bias if you start the interviewing process by phone or by email. Although you may still form judgments based on their voice or choice of words, leaving their physical appearance out of the equation can lend a slightly more neutral perspective. After the first round of vetting through phone calls, you can start bringing candidates in for face-to-face interviews.

Do a Second Interview – Or even a third. You may have missed some red flags in the first interview that are more obvious in the second. Alternatively, you may uncover real potential in a candidate that you overlooked the first time around.

Do a Group Interview – Group interviews can also be helpful to get a different perspective. But at the same time, keep in mind that group interviews are susceptible to "bandwagon" bias. To prevent this, debrief each team member separately to get their honest feedback on the candidate.

Make a Pros and Cons List – A pros and cons list can help ensure you're considering all the factors. Take a hard look at each thing you liked and didn't like and how they would affect job performance. You might find that some of your points don't have anything to do with their ability to do the job well.

Keep an Open Mind – You don't have to discount your intuition entirely, but it is crucial that you don't rush into a hiring decision because you "have a good feeling about them." Ask the right questions and think carefully about their responses. Whenever you have decided you like the candidate, evaluate your reasons why. If it is because of similarity or just because they're likable, be objective about how these factors matter in the position you are hiring them to fill.

Take Detailed Notes – The events we experience are easily twisted by our fallible memory. How we interpret something after the fact might be a far cry from what transpired. You don't need a stenographer to note down every word; even quick bullet points on a notepad should help you keep your facts straight.

CASE STUDY

My Book Editor Checklist

So when I had to rehire a book editor, I put together a checklist. This would serve as a trustworthy guide to be adhered to, irrespective of all the triggers deployed to activate my Bias Codes.

1. Engage, review, assess, and consider a shortlist of at least three high potential editors before making a final hiring decision.

2. Assess for relevant experience and answer the question: Does the editor have verifiable experience editing business books and specifically books in my genre?

3. Find out the top three books they have edited that have been successfully published and get to know what exactly they did with the book. Get testimonials from the authors and any other relevant information.

4. Check references. Find a way to check the references with people whose books they have edited.

5. Do a pilot project. Get them to edit a chapter of the book as proof of competence and base the final hiring decision on the best editing output as well as the customer service experience you had.

6. Check for their ability to work collaboratively on the book-editing project, preferably, one chapter at a time.

7. Check again and again that none of my Bias Codes has been triggered and is driving my selection decision.

Failure is not a sin. Failure to learn from failure, however, is. My experience with the editor that I "hired wrong" was grim, but I've been able to turn the ashes of what was a bitter experience into beauty and learn lessons so I don't ever repeat such mistakes. It should also help others avoid similar mistakes. I will be more cognizant of keeping my Bias Codes in check during the interviewing process!

Thanks to this checklist, I was able to get my book edited to my specifications and expectations. Now, you get to benefit from the book because I made the right hiring decision. Everybody wins.

KEY TAKEAWAYS

- Everybody has a set of biases, which I refer to as their "Bias Code." These can be positive or negative.

- Hiring bias can be a stealthy assassin to your rational thinking. However, knowing what your biases are, and becoming skilled at recognizing them can help you overcome them.

- Solid, objective hiring processes are a powerful antidote to your Bias Code.

- Don't rush hiring. Positive biases can lead to overhasty decision-making.

- Remember the golden rule of hiring: If in doubt, do not hire!

- Whether to spot a potential nightmare employee or to avoid passing over a potentially exceptional employee, stick to your processes and take a step back now and then to consider if you are really as objective as possible.

CHAPTER SIX

VARIETY IS THE SPICE OF HIRING RIGHT

"To such an extent does nature delight and abound in variety that among her trees, there is not one plant to be found which is exactly like another."

Leonardo da Vinci

You should never base your hiring decisions on interviews alone.

Even if you have thoroughly studied the material in the previous chapter about avoiding one's Bias Code, there is always an element of subjectivity in interviews.

Interviews can be "gamed" by smart candidates, who are increasingly often better prepared for interviews than the managers who are supposed to be assessing them!

While hiring managers are taking candidate selection for granted and going through the motions, candidates are preparing like their life depends on it, especially if it is an exciting role within a great organization. I have observed several situations where the candidate appears to want the job more than the hiring manager wants to hire right. Those candidates are going to extreme lengths to prepare to succeed at your interviews. A Google search on how to pass interviews will reveal 511,000,000 (five hundred and eleven million) search results.

Implication: Candidates now have access to a lot of education/information/materials on how to impress and dazzle you at the interview game and pass your interview (whether they are the right candidate for your organization or not). Several smart entrepreneurs are taking advantage of the opportunities created by the desperation of candidates to be successful in the job selection process. They are coming up with creative solutions to give their customers (job seekers) an unfair advantage in the job market.

I recently came across a company that had been set up by ex-employees of the global top four professional services firms. They offer the standard interview coaching and training but also have access to past entrance assessment questions and ideal answers, as well as tips and techniques on what to say or do to succeed during the selection processes of these specific organizations. Using their insider knowledge and experience, they have exposed the selection process and tools the company uses for their most important business activity: hiring!

In my opinion, this is akin to exposing the password to the servers where a company keeps its most important secrets. This practice should never be allowed. However, since there is very little an organization can do about it, the onus is on organizations to do whatever it takes to ensure candidates are unable to "game" their system.

The truth of the matter is that if your organization is one that lots of people would like to work for, knowledge of your hiring process is out there somewhere. You must prepare with this in mind and engage with candidates on the assumption that they have done their homework on you and they know exactly what to expect and they are prepared to tell you precisely what you want to hear so you can hire them. This is one crucial area in which it pays to be paranoid (more about paranoia later: it can be a useful trait!).

Note that this is not a reason not to have a formal hiring process. What you need is to have a set of assessment tools that cannot be gamed, to use alongside interviews.

Another reason for not solely relying on interviews is that they are simply too fallible. Much of what candidates say in interviews is self-reported information about their own competence. Sometimes people tell deliberate lies at interviews, but more often, the untruths are unintended and based on the Dunning-Kruger effect mentioned in the previous chapter. We are simply incapable of assessing our own capabilities accurately. Even when they are morally sound candidates who would never knowingly tell a lie in an interview, they still tend to overestimate their skills. This is as unhelpful as a lie.

One of the ways we have managed to reduce reliance on interviews is by making use of a hiring methodology that we call "A Day in Life." I will use a recent encounter to show it in action.

CASE STUDY

A Day in Life

We wanted to hire a candidate for the Role of Head of E-mail and Content Marketing. One of the candidates interviewed very well. As an added precaution and to ensure we were practicing what we preached, we asked the candidate to come and spend "A Day in Life" with our firm in a bid to simulate what working with us would look like. That way, we would have had the opportunity to see the candidate in his element, working on simulated, scenario-based exercises that sought to replicate actual work.

The day started very well. The candidate arrived on time and was presented with the following brief.

Your CEO has charged you with the responsibility of coming up with:

1. A fit-for-purpose content strategy

2. An integrated email marketing strategy that is a reflection of the diversified business portfolio of the organization

3. A clear description on how you will go about leveraging email for prospecting, outright selling, and contact nurturing

We provided information about the context:

Target Clients

- C-suite, Head of HR & Head of Training

The Nature of Our Business

- B2B professional services firm

Our Marketing Approach

- The marketing approach that has worked for us till now is based on sharing insights and educating our clients

Our Portfolio

- We have several offerings that are diversified but related

We were clear about what we needed and when:

- *Study the above brief thoroughly and ask questions to gain clarification regarding what is expected of you*

- *Engage and consult with all relevant stakeholders such as Business Managers, Client and Industry consultants, Marketing Consultants and Product Managers, to understand their business strategy and ensure your marketing strategy is aligned with this*

- *Put together a PPT presentation detailing exactly how you will fulfill your brief, showcasing samples of email and educational content you will use to engage our clients*

- *You will be required to make a presentation to the CEO and other senior members of the organization between 2–3 p.m.*

He was introduced to a number of individuals within the organization and allowed to ask any questions to seek clarification regarding the brief. He asked a few intelligent-sounding questions, and then said he was ready to begin.

After two hours, the candidate told the coordinator of his Day in Life session that he had changed his mind and was no longer interested in the role. When he was asked why the change of mind, given that he had been involved in the hiring process for almost a month and that this was the last hurdle to cross, he couldn't give any cogent response. His assessor then asked for what he had done in the course of the two hours he had spent on the brief. He couldn't show any work done.

At that point, I was duly informed. My response was, "By all means, he is free to leave the premises and good luck to him on his future endeavors"!

I was more pleased than angry. Yes, we had wasted a lot of time putting this candidate through interviews and other assessments. But imagine if we hadn't taken the candidate through this final process! We would have ended up with a wrong hire and he would have set the organization back significantly. We were much better off with the role vacant than having a less than capable employee occupy it.

Visit **www.hiringrightbook.com** to download a copy of the "A Day in Life" Assessment instrument for your use.

Note how the "A Day in Life" hiring methodology allows us to introduce *peer rating* into our selection process. While the least effective form of rating is self-ratings, peer rating is the most effective.

The most coveted award in club level football is the Players' Player Award, where the other players are the ones to cast the votes. Imagine being asked to vote for another player (apart from yourself, of course) who you believe is the best among the best. Whoever you select will definitely have something significant to offer in terms of capability.

We use this peer rating methodology by asking our employees who are on the same level with candidates we want to hire to interact with these candidates during our Assessment Center process, then to rate their performance as potential peers.

Sometimes we ask the participants in an assessment center vying for the same job to rate each other. The question usually goes like this, "Apart from yourself, which of the other candidates would you rate as highly suitable, based on your interaction with them throughout the day and during the various group exercises? Which candidate would you rank the least?"

We do this with all the candidates, collate the results, and use it as another data point in our selection decision. Most often, the same candidates are ranked among the best three candidates by all their peers. We've never had a situation where a candidate rated by their peers as being unsuitable performed exceptionally well in other forms of assessment.

Peer ratings are, indeed, the most powerful form of assessment.

There are, of course, many other forms of assessment, and new models and ideas keep appearing. Which ones should you use? Rather than give a list of suggestions here (which would soon be out of date), I recommend looking for assessments that have three characteristics. They should be:

- **Reliable.** Does it consistently deliver what it promises?
- **Objective.** Does it transcend biases of various kinds (for example, between candidates of differing race, gender, or nationality)?
- **Valid.** Does it measure what it claims to measure?

As an aside, assessment tools such as the above are not just for use when hiring employees. They are powerful and necessary at all times in the individual's career.

Before an individual is sent for any training, they should have a thorough assessment of what they actually need to learn. Afterward, they should be assessed to evaluate what they have learned.

Assessment is also essential before promotion. X may look like the right candidate for the new post, but the more objectivity you can have about that view, the better. When you have decided, you need to know the "gap" between their current competencies and those that will be required in the new role. How well do they understand the company's products, structures, mission, policies, processes, and procedures?

Quantitative research we conducted among 125 companies revealed that a staggering sixty-four percent of them relied on interviews only for recruitment, and did not use any form of structured assessment at all during their hiring process. Maybe even more surprising, eighty-two percent did not use an assessment for anything other than recruitment purposes. This is setting people up to fail.

Assessments are not only the most potent and valid approach to selecting the right employees; they are also the most effective and efficient methodology for ongoing employee management and development. To significantly increase their probability of hiring right, we believe companies must incorporate relevant assessment instruments into their hiring process.

The Use of Assessment in Hiring - from the Best-Selling Book of All Time

On different occasions, I have stumbled across very interesting, perception-expanding, applications of world-class hiring methodologies while studying the Bible. The two that stood out for me were the accounts in Daniel 1: 1–5 and Judges 7: 1–8 (New International Version).

The fact that the level of sophistication in recruitment and selection captured in the messages existed over 2,500 years ago is not only amazing, but it also proves that the popular saying "There's nothing new under the sun" is indeed true.

Hopefully, after reading my interpretation of these Bible passages, you will be even more convinced about the importance of adopting the right processes when hiring. After all, it was done in the Bible!

Lesson One – Daniel's Recruitment in Babylon (Daniel 1: 1–5)

"In the third year of the reign of Jehoiakim King of Judah,

Nebuchadnezzar King of Babylon came to Jerusalem and besieged it.

And the Lord delivered Jehoiakim King of Judah into his hand, along with some of the articles from the temple of God. These he carried off to the temple of his god in Babylonia[a] and put in the treasure house of his god.

Then the king ordered Ashpenaz, chief of his court officials, to bring in some of the Israelites from the royal family and the nobility—young men without any physical defect, handsome, showing aptitude for every kind of learning, well informed, quick to understand, and qualified to serve in the king's palace. He was to teach them the language and literature of the Babylonians.

The king assigned them a daily amount of food and wine from the king's table. They were to be trained for three years, and after that they were to enter the king's service."

The person specifications contained in the brief that the king gave to Ashpenaz, his Head of HR, are very instructive. This ruler from 2,500 years ago was much more competent in communicating his hiring needs precisely than most CEOs we have come across in recent years!

Below is an analysis of the king's non-negotiable hiring requirements and my amateur take on the reasoning behind his person specification.

S/No	Person Specification (The King's Non-Negotiables	Justification	Implications for 21st Century Organizations
1	Royal Family and the nobility	The newly hired candidates will be serving the king and hence, it was critical for them to come from a similar background.	When it comes to hiring right, "fit" matters a lot, and organizations must ensure that they do everything possible to hire people who are appropriate for their specific context.
2	Young men without any physical defect	The role required people who were physically fit and appealing to compliment the "look and feel" of the palace so the king could "show off" to his visitors, which was a critical requirement of the royals. They needed to look good in front of visitors to the palace.	This specification would be adjudged to be discriminatory and politically incorrect in the current dispensation. However, the role's requirement was essential. Where it is verifiable that the specification is a necessity (and not some bias-motivated condition), this sort of specification is important.

3	Showing aptitude for every kind of learning	The king expected the right candidates to have high learning agility. They had to be capable of learning and acquiring critical competencies that would enable them to excel in their new role.	Aptitude testing is crucial in the selection process. In the 21st century, learning agility is even more critical, as organizations are required to outlearn their competitors if they expect to survive and thrive. We must assess a potential employee's aptitude for learning.
4	Well informed	The king expected the right candidates to have high learning agility. They had to be capable of learning and acquiring critical competencies that would enable them to excel in their new role.	Aptitude testing is crucial in the selection process. In the 21st century, learning agility is even more critical, as organizations are required to outlearn their competitors if they expect to survive and thrive. We must assess a potential employee's aptitude for learning.
5	Quick to understand	The king wanted candidates who could learn very fast. Considering the magnitude of expectations from the candidates regarding the role they would be playing, this was of critical importance.	This is related to learning agility and aptitude for a range of learning, as discussed above. There is a strong positive correlation between high learning agility and superior performance on the job.
6	Qualified to serve in the King's palace	Serving in the king's palace was not for everyone. It was the highest career aspiration possible and you had to be qualified to be chosen to serve at the highest level.	Qualifications play a significant role in ensuring that organizations have people with know-how and competence to excel in specific roles. Organizations must establish the criteria required for success in each critical role and ensure they are making selection decisions based on the established requirements.
7	Teach them Language and Literature	The two core competencies required for serving in the royal palace were language and literature.	Every organization must identify its core competencies, i.e., those competencies that their success and business continuity are hinged upon. They must then ensure that every single member of the organization, irrespective of their role, acquires a certain level of proficiency in those competencies.

			Examples of Core Competencies include Project Management, Presentation Skills and being Customer Centric.
8	Trained for three years	The culture in the palace was critical to the continuity of the royal dynasty. Even though the candidates had all the other qualities described above, they still had to go through three years of induction and acculturation.	Employee induction is one of the most critical activities that an organization can use to increase its probability of success. Sadly, this critical intervention is "hit or miss" in most organizations. Sometimes new employee induction is left to chance and organizations miss an excellent opportunity to help their new hire hit the ground running. How long is your Employee Induction Program? In the elite organization of the king's palace, 2,500 years ago, induction was for three years. You could argue of course that the candidates couldn't be poached as they were not allowed to resign—and you would be absolutely right. However, the quality of Employee Induction is too important to be left to chance.
9	Enter the King's Service	It was only when all the non-negotiables were in place that the candidates could be allowed to enter into the king's service.	Companies must raise the bar when it comes to hiring people. Because hiring right is a matter of life and death, it should be easier for a camel to pass through the eye of the needle than for a new hire to be recruited into your organization.

Lesson Two - Gideon Defeats the Midianites (Judges 7: 1–8)

"Early in the morning, Jerub-Baal (that is, Gideon) and all his men camped at the spring of Harod. The camp of Midian was north of them in the valley near the hill of Moreh.

The LORD said to Gideon, "You have too many men for me to deliver Midian into their hands. In order that Israel may not boast against me that her own strength has saved her, announce now to the people, 'Anyone who trembles with fear may turn back and leave Mount Gilead.'" So 22,000 men left, while 10,000 remained.

But the LORD said to Gideon, "There are still too many men. Take them down to the water, and I will sift them for you there. If I say, "This one shall go with you," he shall go; but if I say, "This one shall not go with you," he shall not go."

So Gideon took the men down to the water. There the LORD told him, "Separate those who lap the water with their tongues like a dog from those who kneel down to drink."

Three hundred men lapped with their hands to their mouths.

All the rest got down on their knees to drink.

The LORD said to Gideon, "With the 300 men that lapped I will save you and give the Midianites into your hands. Let all the other men go, each to his own place." So Gideon sent the rest of the Israelites to their tents but kept the 300, who took over the provisions and trumpets of the others."

When it comes to winning the business war, the above example is better than any I have seen in *Harvard Business Review*: in fact, it is mind-boggling in its implication. This is the best of Assessment and Development Center in action! If you find yourself wishing that God would still speak directly to mere mortals like us, you are not alone. However, regarding your talent, God has said all he needs to say. The question is, are you going to learn from the different lessons and case studies demonstrating what you need to do to win the war for talent?

Frequently, I come across business owners and executives who readily concede to the fact that they have made poor hiring decisions in the past that are hunting them presently, and they want to know what to do. The answer can be found in this bible passage.

If you find your organization in a situation where prior wrong hiring decisions have put a lid on your growth potential or worse, are gradually eroding value, the best remedy will be to apply the principles shared in this chapter. You need to carry out a practical staff competency audit to determine the capability gaps that exist in your organization. Depending on the extent of the gaps, you might not have much choice than to ask the employees that are unfit to "turn back and go home."

What about training and development? This is a question I have heard several times. Why don't we invest in developing these non-performing employees to improve their performance?

One standard HR response to this is that such people need to be "developed." This is true in an ideal world, but in tough, competitive markets, development itself needs to be targeted on the people with the most potential. If people lack this potential, they are best "let go" (in a pleasant, civilized way, of course).

My best response to this is succinctly captured by Paul Russell's quote below;

"Development can help great people be even better—but if I had a dollar to spend, I'd spend 70 cents getting the right person in the door."

The training and development of employees is a valuable activity that an organization can invest in as it has the potential to create unmatched competitive advantage when it is the appropriate solution. Sadly, there is a considerable limitation to this approach. If the challenge is 'fit', development is often not the right solution. It is much more expedient to ensure you have the right people in the right roles and then train them to be the best they can possibly be.

Below is my additional analysis of this profoundly simple Bible passage.

"You have too many men." Sadly, in many of the organizations, we have encountered in the course of our consulting engagements, this is the case. Most organizations are bloated and have very few wealth-creating people contributing to its real value (The 80/20 principle is definitely at play). A sizeable proportion of the people in these organizations are "paid audiences"—people who are being paid by you to watch you (the executive) do the job you are paying them to do.

Many of the executives we come across are burnt-out, overwhelmed, stressed, overworked, and un-strategic (in other words, unable to play the strategic role that their organization desperately needs for them to play) because of the extra work they have to do to make up for "passengers" in their organization. Most organizations need to streamline—go lean and mean. They need a scientific methodology to assess and ensure their people are battle-ready and have the capabilities required to win in the marketplace. The methodology is that of the Assessment and Development Center.

"Anyone who trembles with fear may turn back and leave." If you have too many employees, you need to create incentives for excess staff to leave voluntarily. This can be easy for large and buoyant companies but is unrealistic for medium to small organizations that are fighting for their survival. Asking people to leave your organization voluntarily might have worked 2,500 years ago in the Bible, but it's highly unlikely that it will work in the 21st century. You need to evolve a methodology for getting rid of people who are not a "fit" for the business. A Staff Competency Audit enables you to do this. Your organization must "Sift for Fit." This requires an in-depth understanding of what is needed for success in the role. Without this understanding, it is impossible to screen and sift for people with the potential to succeed in the role from those who do not.

The criterion chosen by God is also very relevant. It was a mental one, not a skill-based one. It is not enough to have people with the right competencies. People have to have the right spirit. The journey to business success can be a hard one, and if people lack the passion and "can-do" attitude, they can be baggage on that journey, dragging the organization down. Skills, after all, can be learned, especially by bright, able people. The right attitude is a much harder thing to acquire.

"Separate those who lap the water with their tongues like a dog from those who kneel to drink." Having got rid of people with the wrong mindset, it was then time to sift for skill. Even here, however, the assessment wasn't about simple technical skills, but about general savvy, about agility and alertness. In this case, the people who lapped the water weren't sharp enough for the task in hand.

By bending down and lapping, they took their concentration away from the environment and put it all on the water. Those who cupped their hands and drank could remain upright and keep scanning the environment about them for any kind of threat. They "kept their eyes on the ball." They would be ready to move at a moment's notice.

In modern business, the equivalent is the critical ability to keep a range of issues in mind and not putting all of one's attention on one issue.

This assessment methodology was also pragmatic and straightforward. It was reliable—it would always sift out the same people. It was objective—it made no concessions to biases. It was valid—it selected for what it meant to select for. It left no doubt that the people chosen had the competencies that matched what was required for success.

Another key lesson to be gotten from this bible passage is the classic strategy move leading organizations adopt when they are experiencing business decline. Popularly referred to as **"Shrinking to Grow,"** it is the go-to-strategy for turning around a business that is experiencing decline or stagnation. Several best-in-class organizations, including Apple, Microsoft, P&G, etc. have adopted the Strategy of Shrinking to Grow to successfully turn around the fortune of their companies.

Sometimes organizations must shrink to grow. It is necessary for focus and effectiveness. And just as losing weight while developing your muscle is the key to attaining physical fitness and good health, companies need to shed employees that are not a fit to enable them to focus and win with the right people. Just like Gideon did.

"Where quality matters, quantity can never be an effective substitute"

Gideon, by the way, defeated his enemy. They crept up on the encamped Midianites by night, lit lamps, blew horns, and shouted war cries. The enemy thought they had been surprised by a huge army and fled in confusion.

Organizations can learn a lot from this simple yet powerful principle of ensuring you have the right people for the right context. An organization at war, fighting for its very survival, needs warriors—people who have what it takes mentally and emotionally to win in the marketplace. A well-orchestrated process for ensuring that you have the right people with you is absolutely non-negotiable.

Whatever You Do, Make Sure You Check References

This is another essential part of the hiring mix. It is too risky to make a hiring decision, especially for a critical role, without carrying out reference checks on the candidate to be hired. But people still do this: often when they are full of excitement that, after a "perfect" interview, they have found just the right person!

A friend (who is also a business owner and CEO) recently had his HR department source and hire a candidate for the role of CFO but neglected to check the candidate's reference. Bad mistake.

He ended up firing the candidate within two weeks because he caught the candidate recording their conversation on his phone. On asking the candidate why he was recording their conversation without permission (which, by the way, is illegal), the candidate claimed that he always recorded conversations with his bosses in case a dispute arose in the future and he needed to clear himself. Yes, you read that right. That was his exact response!

Of course, the CEO fired him immediately. When the CEO shared his experience with me, I asked him to go and check the candidate's references. I told him it was vital that he ensured that the lesson learned from the experience was complete and this would not be the case if he didn't follow through and check the fired employee's reference.

What he discovered made him break out in a cold sweat. The candidate had been fired from his previous place of employment and had tried to use the conversations he recorded to get his last boss into trouble with the board of directors and their industry regulator.

It also turned out that the individual was psychologically imbalanced and had major anger issues. The CEO would have had this knowledge before hiring the candidate if only he had bothered to check the reference. I can assure you this CEO will never hire another employee again without checking their references.

However, most traditional methods of checking references are not sufficient, considering what is at stake. In addition to what companies currently do, I will highly recommend informal, one-on-one, targeted reference checking, employing a 360-degree approach.

A 360-degree feedback intervention is a process where superiors, peers, direct reports, and sometimes, customers evaluate an individual. The benefit of collecting data of this kind is that the employee gets to see a panorama of perceptions rather than just self-perception or a possibly biased view from a line manager. This affords a more thorough feedback about the employee. The same principle can be used in obtaining references. A 360-degree reference checking approach delivers the best results every time.

To use this approach, identify the candidate's former bosses, peers, and direct reports and crosscheck references to have a holistic view of the candidate. What are their bosses' impression of them? What do their peers think of their effectiveness? How do their direct reports view their leadership capabilities?

The more informal you can make these checks, the better. This is not always easy to do, as the people being questioned might not know you. But it is worth making an effort to find past and present co-workers who will tell you what they really think.

The problem is that genuine opinions, if negative, rarely find their ways into formal references. Referees don't want to be seen to speak ill of people and are afraid of legal consequences if they are negative about someone (however poor that person has been at their job).

It is often only through this informal system that you get a true picture of an individual. Do they really deliver results, or piggyback on other's achievements? How are they as colleagues? Are they helpful? Do they exchange ideas and information? Are they great teammates or "lone wolves"? As leaders, do they care about the individuals as well as driving performance? Or are they dictators? The more information you seek out, the greater your chances of avoiding a painful, costly mistake.

There is an ancient cowboy saying that if one person calls you a horse, the person is crazy. If three people call you a horse, it's a conspiracy/gang-up of some sort against you. But if ten people call you a horse, it's time to consider buying a saddle. 360 degrees reference checking is extremely invaluable because it captures the feedback on an individual from diverse perspectives, and should be incorporated into your organization's hiring practice.

CASE STUDY

How an Informal Reference Check Saved the Day

The candidate, for a key post had performed well at the interview and looked excellent from a set of psychometric tests. The individual's experience was right, and the qualifications looked good (and genuine: we checked). However, something inside me still felt wrong. (Note that there is still a role for "gut feel" in hiring. This book is not about how to completely remove intuition from the hiring process, but about how to put it in a structural context.)

For various reasons, I didn't want to contact his current employer. I looked at his CV and identified his employer before the current one. I found out the name of the CEO of that organization at that time (the person was still performing that role).

Rather than simply ring this busy CEO up, I asked around my network of friends and contacts to see if anyone knew him. One of them did, and I asked him to introduce me to the CEO, which he did. When I called the CEO up, he knew who I was and was happy to talk to me.

I said that I wanted, informally, to talk about the candidate. I insisted that the conversation was "off the record," and he double-checked that. Once he trusted that the conversation would be totally confidential, he told me not to hire the person. The candidate was very able, but had a negative attitude to the job, being only interested in what he could get out of the organization and giving as little as he could get away with.

His former CEO also said that the candidate was very good at claiming credit for the achievements of other people. This type of person is particularly difficult to spot at interview or by a formal referencing system, where it often looks like they are a high achiever. In fact, it is people around them who have achieved, but this individual has been skilled at appropriating their accomplishments. This trait may be spotted during "A Day in Life," sessions – but informal discussions with former co-workers are often the best way. And of course, such information is pure gold for the hirer.

Just to emphasize the point in this story, the 'gut feeling' followed several formal processes, and was only acted upon by using another process. It played a role in the hiring process, but it wasn't a substitute for it. In the end, the decision was an easy one, requiring no soul-searching

In God we trust. All others bring data."

W. Edwards Deming

KEY TAKEAWAYS

- Job seekers are getting smarter and more desperate to get their dream jobs. They will do whatever they can to enter the work system. To counter this, managers must ensure they prepare adequately for candidate selection.

- Bias in interviews never totally goes away.

- Self-rating is the least effective form of assessment and not reliable. Some candidates lie, but even honest ones tend to overrate their skill and achievements at interviews.

- As a result of the above, interviews should not be used as a sole means of assessing candidates.

- There are many other types of assessment methods. Use them.

- "A Day in Life" tool is an excellent way of testing the true mettle of a candidate.

- Peer rating is a highly effective assessment tool. Organizations should find ways to incorporate it into their hiring process.

- Organizations must check candidates' references, especially when recruiting for critical roles.

- The best reference checks are informal conversations, as people are often very unwilling to put negative comments in formal references for fear of personal revenge or legal consequences.

- I highly recommend that organizations take assessment lessons from the bestselling book of all time!

CHAPTER SEVEN

LACK OF ACCOUNTABILITY

"What you cannot measure, you cannot manage
What you cannot manage, you cannot improve
What you cannot improve, cannot create sustainable value
What cannot create sustainable value cannot grow
What cannot grow will die eventually."

Anonymous

This chapter may be short, but its message is crucial.

To ensure your company hires right, you must set clear metrics and hold the people involved with hiring accountable to these metrics. There should be an appropriate consequence management policy in place around your hiring practices.

Many a time, I have come across organizations that only measure the speed of hiring instead of dealing with infinitely more important measures that relate to the quality of hiring. This, of course, is not right.

A useful comparison is with a fund management company. If you, as a portfolio manager, consistently pick the wrong stocks, you will not last long. The fact that you picked the stocks quickly wouldn't make any difference to this. The same should be true of managers picking team members.

I suggest having these metrics in place:

1. The degree of the manager's compliance with the company's hiring standards and processes
2. Quality of the candidate as a measure of their performance during the selection process
3. The quality of the candidate hired (to be determined after the six-month probation period, based on their performance in their role). This is the most telling metric of all. If you want to keep your system simple, make this the one non-negotiable target for hiring managers.
4. Percentage of candidates rejected at the next/higher level in the recruitment process
5. Number of candidates that turned the offer down and the reason why they did
6. Candidates' rating of the end-to-end hiring experience
7. Number of candidates shortlisted and taken through the hiring process

I rarely see such lists in small- or medium-sized companies (world-class ones are different). As a result, in these organizations the old maxim asserts itself, that "what gets measured gets done, and what doesn't get measured doesn't get done." Managers whose KPIs don't include the above rush through the hiring process.

They can't really be blamed for this. They're busy and have other pressures, other targets to meet. Many managers are only assessed on how much revenue they bring in over a quarter (or some similar time-period). Longer-term issues such as Hiring Right are ignored.

Of course, it is only a matter of time before these poor hiring practices start causing difficulties.

Listed below are simple steps you can take to ensure this does not happen:

1. Train all managers in hiring. That way, they will not only do the job better, but they will also feel happier being assessed on the quality of their hires. It is, after all, unfair to assess people on how they do something they haven't been trained on how to do.
2. Select some managers, the best at hiring (see Chapter Four), and make this a major part of their responsibility.
3. Make hiring a key part of every (or at least most) managers' responsibilities.
4. Have KPIs linked to the list above. If you are to pick one KPI out of that list, make it number three. The performance of the hired individual(s) after a period of time – six months or a year is a good length – is probably the best measure of the quality of a hire.

Behind all this, of course, is the matter of culture, which is driven from the top. If the CEO takes their time to pick the best people, the rest of the team will do the same. If, when someone pulls off some amazing piece of work, the leader not only congratulates them, but also gives appropriate recognition to the person who appointed them for getting it right, hiring will become more and more respected as an activity.

CASE STUDY

Hiring Managers Get into Trouble for past Hiring Decision

In response to a more competitive financial services market, our client, Bank X, engaged our services as part of their efforts to strategically improve the effectiveness, efficiency and profitability of their branch networks.

With the recognition that branches play a major role in the delivery of business volume, and consequently, have a significant impact on the performance of the bank as a whole; the bank identified the need to have the right leadership at the branch levels.

Due to the strategic nature of the role, the bank needed managers who were capable of managing the end-to-end activities of their branches for optimum performance.

The starting point was to ask and answer the following questions;

- Do the bank's current branch managers have the critical competencies required to run their branches successfully?

- If there are competency gaps, what are they? Can these gaps be closed easily?

- Who are the best-performing branch managers and what are their differentiating competencies?

- Can what the best performing managers know and do be studied, codified, documented and shared to improve performance across the bank?

To answer the first question, we organized an assessment center to evaluate the suitability of the current branch managers to effectively run their branches.

The assessment center was quite revealing as we were able to identify superstar-branch managers and those that didn't have what it took to succeed.

There was a particularly poor performance report for one of the branch managers. The report was so abysmal that the CEO, who was part of the assessment panel kept on insisting that he was sure the branch manager was not a valid member of staff.

Lo and behold, he requested to see the staff file to ascertain the following;

- The validity of the manager's claim that he was actually a member of staff
- The names of the hiring managers responsible for the hire

Not only did the hiring managers receive a query for their hiring decision, but they also had to undergo a compulsory hiring training program, before they could be allowed to recruit for the organization again.

Subsequently, the CEO ordered the complete overhauling of the hiring process of the organization and made it compulsory for all hiring managers to be held accountable for their hiring decisions.

You are only as good as the people that report to you. If you do not insist on hiring absolutely the best, then you are consciously deciding that employees of average or worse quality are acceptablee."

David Forman, HCI

KEY TAKEAWAYS

- Where hiring right is concerned, accountability and right metrics are non-negotiable.
- The Key Performance Indicators of line managers must reflect the importance of the role they play in hiring activities. Simply to reward managers by the amount of revenue their departments bring in is dangerous short-term thinking.
- There are a number of metrics used for measuring hiring success. Speed of hiring is the worst.
- Make sure everyone in the company knows the importance of hiring right so that people will accept and understand their "hiring" KPIs.

CHAPTER EIGHT

LACK OF RESOURCES

"Time spent on hiring is time well spent"
Robert Half

This is another brief chapter, but as with Chapter Seven, its message is extremely important. It may not be a complex issue, but I have seen many businesses fail to hire right because they make the elementary mistake of not allocating enough resources to the process.

Resource allocation often falls foul of the "triangle of death":

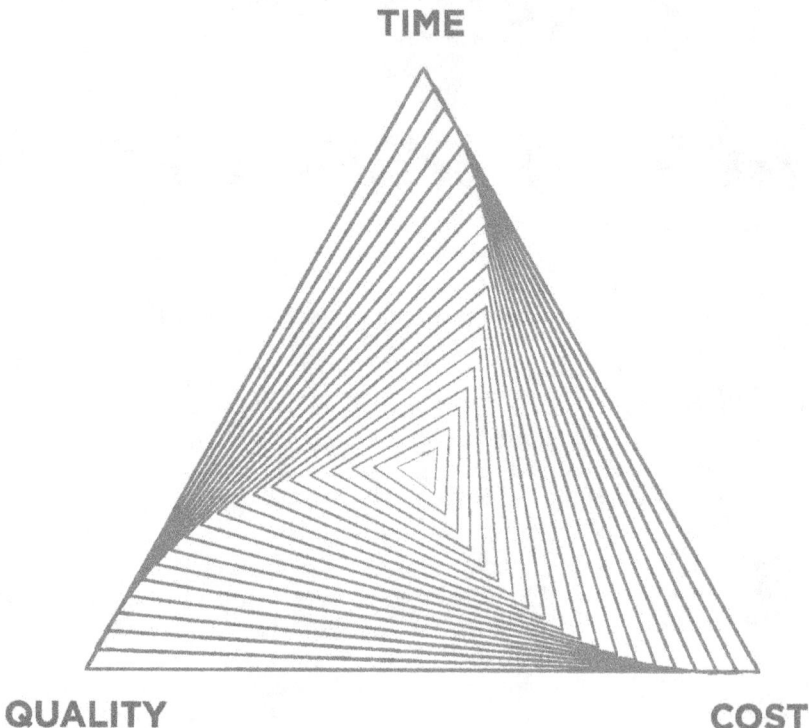

TIME

QUALITY   **COST**

Trying to get one of these right creates pressure on the other two. Given that quality is non-negotiable, the only way to keep the triangle in shape is to spend resources on the other two corners as well. Hiring right requires rigor, attention to details, and dedication. And in turn, these require adequate resources like time, money, location, the right tools and most importantly, the right people. To ensure hiring success, these must be assured, period.

Time

I have already criticized some managers for not devoting enough time to hiring, a problem that is made clear when they leaf through a pile of CVs and ask the newly arrived candidate to repeat their name several times. "Ah, yes," they say as they find the right CV, and then "Hmmm" as they read it for the first time.

Interviewing requires time, as does hiring generally, and time is one of the scarcest resources in most organizations. This often represents a major challenge. Organizations must plan in such a way so that adequate time is dedicated to hiring right. The ability to plan a recruitment process and avoid hiring under pressure is crucial. Making hiring decisions in a hurry is dangerous to the health and well-being of organizations and should be avoided at all costs.

Location

Managers should not be allowed to conduct the hiring process from behind their work desks. The temptation to continue reading and responding to their emails or answering their phone can be difficult for them to resist. Simply put, these distractions reduce the quality of the hiring process.

To avoid distraction, dedicated meeting rooms should be used for hiring. If there is no space free among your own offices, rent one. There are plenty of companies selling office space by the day or even the hour. They will provide a decent room with essential facilities and (usually) refreshments. Some of our clients leave their offices and come to ours.

If the position under consideration is a senior one, a good hotel is a better location. A smart hotel sends a message to the candidates that you are serious, that you respect them, and that you don't starve important projects of resources. It also gives you the chance to observe candidates without distraction.

Don't conduct interviews at a desk. A good interviewing space is two chairs at an angle to each other. Face to face interviews may seem confrontational.

Budget

Adequate budget must be allocated for hiring to ensure its success. This must cover items such as assessment instruments and logistics such as the hotel in the example above.

You may wish to outsource all or part of the process to a capable hiring agency. As I run such an organization, I would naturally say that—but consider the facts objectively! Good outsourced hirers know what assessment tools to use and how to get them at a sensible price. They have deals with major hotels and office-space providers. They have access to the market, with a wide range of candidates on their books. Above all, they are experienced—recruitment is what they do day in and day out. They will form part of your process, or create their own, and will make sure it all works as smoothly and effectively as possible.

Hiring the right agency can be an excellent investment.

People

The right people are the ones that can hire right. As the saying goes, you can't give what you don't have. Your best people must be the ones charged with the responsibility of making selection and hiring decisions on behalf of your organization. This is why I recommend that organizations should have designated interviewers/hiring managers who have been well trained or certified on the company's hiring process. Hiring is a huge responsibility and cannot be delegated to just anyone who happens to be less busy or available at a particular moment.

Designated Hiring Managers (DHM) must be selected with the utmost care. The quality time they will be required to dedicate to hiring right must be factored into their workload. They should be compensated for the hiring work they do. This is critical if you are going to build a successful organization.

Even though hiring right is a joint responsibility of both the line managers and the HR function, line managers must take ownership of the hiring process. HR should provide support as well as ensure compliance with laid-down processes and standards. We have come across instances where line managers abdicate responsibility for hiring and leave it in the total control of HR. This shouldn't be the case.

Ultimately, line managers own talent issues and hence, must own the talent process. HR is there to play the role of an enabler and enforcer of the hiring process. This is a major reason why the managers' KPIs must contain hiring metrics.

KEY TAKEAWAYS

- Adequate time, budget, people, location, and other resources must be allocated to the hiring process to ensure success.
- The process must be planned: having to rush this most important of decisions is not conducive to good choices.
- Interviews should not be carried out in managers' offices, where there are too many distractions.
- For senior appointments, a top-class hotel is the best location.
- The key is to have designated interviewers with their workload and benefits reflecting the fact that they have this critically important responsibility.
- Consider involving an external consultant in your major hiring decisions. They add expertise and objectivity.

CHAPTER NINE

GREAT TALENT, NOT ENOUGH TO GO ROUND

"If I were running a company today, I would have one priority above all others: to acquire as many of the best people as I could [because] the single biggest constraint on the success of my organization is the ability to get and to hang on to enough of the right people."

Jim Collins

When was the last time you felt like you were scrambling to fill critical but vacant roles in your organization? How many times have you experienced increasing difficulty with filling critical roles and eventually having to settle for someone who didn't really have the skills to succeed? When you take a cross-sectional look across your organization in its current state, how different is it from the lineup you had a year ago?

According to a 2018 talent shortage survey by Manpower Group, forty-five percent of employers worldwide had trouble filling vacant roles within their company. That's a fourteen percent increase in ten years. At this rate, tens of millions of jobs will go unfilled over the next decade, resulting in trillions of dollars in lost revenue. The mismatch between talent and skill requirements is at an all-time high.

The quality of your hiring ultimately depends on the quality of the pool of people that you can attract to your organization. Sadly, the growing shortage of talent makes this pool ever harder to create. This is a problem globally, but the picture in many parts of the world, including, sadly, Africa, is even uglier due to the "brain drain" as talents find overseas opportunities attractive.

What are the factors responsible for this crisis? There are no less than eight of them:

1. **Globalization** – Thanks to the constant advancement of technologies, communication and transportation, the world is becoming more connected. This is admirable in some ways, but it has resulted in a severely disproportionate allocation of talents.

    I can conduct a business meeting with someone who is halfway around the world or place an order for a product made hundreds of miles away and have it delivered to my front door tomorrow. Great!

    But globalization means that the best talent isn't bound to the city, or even the country, they live in. These days, the best talent can secure work virtually anywhere by working remotely.

2. **Greater competition** – If you have put out a job advert to hire for a mid-level or senior role in the last couple of years, you've likely experienced one of these two situations:

    a) You received so few applications that you wondered if you put the wrong contact email address in the job posting.

    b) You are inundated with applications but more than ninety percent of the applicants are missing key qualifications.

There are now more jobs than there is talent, resulting in fewer relevant applications. Gone are the days when talented individuals will come knocking at your door. Instead, all organizations are vying for the same top candidates.

And it's not just candidates "out there" who are being snapped up by the competition. Your competitors are likely soliciting your *current* employees under your nose with offers of higher pay and better titles. Employees will resign, seemingly out of the blue, only for their LinkedIn profile to suddenly deliver the news that they have ended up at a rival company, with all your trade secrets and strategic knowledge.

3. **Aging workforce** – With baby-boomers now between the ages of 55 and 75, there is a noticeable surge in retirements, with about 10,000 occurring every day.

    This staggering volume of seniors hanging up their neckties is expected to continue for the next eleven years. The incoming generations are fewer in number and aren't learning or growing fast enough to fill this expanding gap. So, the top talent pool is shrinking while the demand for skills and expertise is rising.

    Many of these retiring baby boomers are in higher-level positions and have decades of experience. They leave behind big shoes for the subsequent generations to fill, even for those who have the relevant post-secondary education; in so many ways, education and training can't substitute for experience.

4. **Quality of education and preparedness for the job market** – The overall quality of education worldwide has succumbed to a noticeable decline over the years. Literacy and math skills have been plummeting since the early nineties. Grade inflation is another worrying concern that has been noticed by educational experts.

    There is a rise in the number of high school students being awarded an A average, yet sinking SAT/JAMB scores tell a different story. Similarly, universities are witnessing an inexplicable spike in the number of students who are graduating with first- and upper-second-class degrees that they cannot defend. Academic standards are wavering.

    For the last decade, adults have been entering the workforce without the same quality of education as the preceding generation. As if that isn't concerning enough, the costs of post-secondary education have skyrocketed. For example, the cost of university tuition fees in the U.K. has increased threefold in the past decade. Interest on loans to U.K. students can be as high as six percent, despite the country's bank rate being 0.25%. This has led many high-school graduates to opt-out of post-secondary education, choosing instead to look for work right out of high school, which further limits the skills available in the talent pool.

5. **Rapidly Developing Technologies** – Tech isn't just an industry anymore; it's a requirement within every industry and every business. And it's developing so rapidly that we can't keep up. Even those who are already working in the tech and IT sectors are feeling the pressure to try and acquaint themselves with each new technological innovation being introduced to businesses.

    There's a need like never before for expertise in data analysis, software engineering, cybersecurity, and programming, because nearly every business under the sun needs some sort of IT in order to stay competitive and keep growing. Here, more than anywhere else is the pinch point. While mid-management roles in these sectors are difficult to fill, most organizations have trouble filling roles for even the junior-level specialists in them.

6. **Migration Trends** – Everyday droves of skilled workers emigrate from lower-resource countries to better paying and more developed societies, seeking greener pastures and further shrinking the already small talent pool in their native countries.

7. **The Changing Economy** – When the Great Recession hit in 2008, layoffs and mergers left more workers than jobs. If companies did need to hire, they had their pick from the pool of talented individuals who were desperate for a paycheck.

    More than ten years later, the economy has bounced back and there are now more jobs coming onto the market than there are people to fill them. Unemployment levels across the globe are at an all-time low as businesses are rapidly expanding. Ironically, our economic recovery could be the very thing that spurs the next global recession if we aren't able to fill these jobs and keep our businesses growing.

    All the above are issues that affect everyone on a global scale.

However, there are things you can do to prevent talent shortage within your own business. You can consistently hire the right "fit" employee from the shrinking pool of right talent available in your marketplace. We have helped many organizations do this.

To achieve this feat consistently, companies adopt four broad tactics:

a) Pay for quality
b) Grow your talent
c) Have a powerful EVP (Employee Value Proposition)
d) Always be in the market looking for talent

"The secret of my success is that we have gone to exceptional lengths to hire the best people in the world."

Steve Jobs

A single "right fit" employee is better than ten average ones. Whatever you do, avoid compromising on the quality of your new hires. I have personally realized that some roles are so critical to the success of my company that we are better off if those roles remain vacant rather than to have employees who are not a 'fit' in those roles. In our company, we have had to learn this principle the hard way and we have the battle scars to show for our mistakes. The value of the right person, especially in a critical role, is just too important to leave to chance.

From my experience, the main reason that small- to medium-sized, owner-led organizations hesitate to pay a premium for the "right fit" employee is because there is no guarantee regarding employee performance. Memories of bad past hiring experiences prevent companies from reaching into their pockets and paying extra for what seem to be top people. "Supposing we get it wrong again?"

Organizations must be willing to take calculated risks in this area. The way to hedge your risk is by fixing your hiring process and your performance management system.

If you take a candidate through a well-defined and expertly designed rigorous hiring process, which validates that the candidate is the right fit for the role, you should be willing to take the risk and then leverage your performance management system to manage that risk (Exactly how you do that is beyond the scope of this book).

There are simply no guarantees in life and business. Waking up every day and driving to work is a risk. You mitigate that risk by using your seat belt, staying alert, and concentrating on your driving. With the right organizational culture and management system, you can effectively manage the right person for value. If you are a bit skeptical about this, I don't blame you; but for the sake of your business and its survival, you will have to take the risk and do whatever is necessary to attract the right talent.

One of my colleagues shared a formula with me, which, according to him, was used by a successful and famous CEO. The title of the formula is one, two, three. Here is the definition:

- ✓ Hire *one* right fit employee
- ✓ Pay her the salary of *two* people
- ✓ Get her to do the job of *three* people

It's worth considering implementing this formula in your organization. If you have to, leverage to pay the right talent. It is that important.

CASE STUDY

Doing Whatever It Takes To Get The Best Person

A while ago, one of our clients engaged our hiring services with a brief to assist the company in hiring a top candidate for a very critical technical role. We identified several candidates during the search engagement, but one of them stood out distinctively.

During the interview stage of the hiring process, the COO, who was heading the interview panel, excused himself halfway through the interview to go out and place a call to the CEO of the company with the message, "You absolutely have to meet with this amazing candidate today." The CEO agreed and rearranged his calendar to accommodate the request.

The candidate had experience with regard to the two big technical challenges then facing the company—not only of meeting these challenges but of solving them. She knew exactly what the company needed to do and could do it.

After interviewing the candidate, the CEO requested that she stay in town until the next day – she had flown in from another state. He booked her into a five-star hotel and asked her to put together a presentation on her approach for solving the two technical problems and present it to him and a few members of the board of the company by noon the following day.

The presentation went so well the next day that the candidate was offered double what she was currently earning, with accommodation provided as part of the benefits (she would be relocating to a new state). She accepted.

Later that day, she made the same presentation to a group of investors and their bankers and the company was able to secure the investment they needed for the expansion of their technical operations. The new arrival had earned her extra salary already.

That is the potential the right person has and can bring to the table. The CEO told me six months later that hiring her was the single most crucial business decision he had made that year. Such is the power of hiring right—but it can sometimes take decisiveness and "thinking big" financially to bring this power to bear.

Grow Your Talent

Another tactic that has been very successful for addressing the shortage of the right people is the commitment to growing your own talent. We have used this tactic for ourselves and on behalf of our clients to gain hard-to-duplicate competitive advantage.

The process involves getting your own training academy focused on identifying, selecting, and developing fresh graduates or candidates with two to three years of work experience. We have two schemes, one for new graduates and one for people with some experience within the organization.

The academy is not cheap. It takes up resources of money, time, effort, attention, and space. But these are the best investments an organization can make for its future. Your company will be building your talent and the future leaders of the organization.

Your academy can be a mixture of classroom, online study, and on-the-job training. It can be a mixture of basic office and commercial training, and training that is specific to your organization and industry.

Growing talent isn't just about new or recent arrivals. Senior workers who are nearing retirement age should mentor the people likely to replace them.

Growing your talent at all levels can be a huge advantage over time, enabling you to shape the behavior of your employees to align with your organizational culture—and keeping them involved, interested, and committed to you.

CASE STUDY

Growing Your Own Talent

One of our clients, a clear leader in its industry and one of the most successful companies we work with, has a phenomenal "Grow Your Own Talent" program right at the center of its highly successful human capital strategy . This program has been very successful indeed and it is regarded as the key element in the strong culture and excellent business results that the company has enjoyed over the past two decades.

The Grow Your Own Talent practice at this organization involves a very rigorous, standardized induction process lasting four to six months.

The effects of the program reach far up the company. Even with the highest-level jobs, the company prefers to promote from its homegrown talent pool than to adopt the practice of parachuting talent into senior positions from outside. Such is the quality and standard of the program that candidates who fail to graduate from it successfully are quickly snapped up by the company's competitors.

One aspect of the company's program that we find particularly refreshing and life-transforming is the habit of discipline that the company develops in the participants, which we believe is pivotal considering the age of these graduates. On one particular occasion, the company canceled and rejected an entire cohort of academy participants due to actions the company deemed unacceptable just a day before graduation. The cohort was full of bright people but difficult to manage. Things came to a head when a couple of them went missing from a critical class. These missing delegates appeared halfway through, and were not allowed in as a punishment—after that most of the class walked out. They were all told that their attitude was not wanted in the company, despite the company having invested millions in the program. Frankly, I don't know of many organizations that would do that.

Another interesting thing about the academy is the fact that while in it, participants are paid but not provided lunch. This practice stems from the belief that the participants are co-investors in their own personal development and careers, and their equity contribution to the journey is paying for their lunch. This is a bold decision and one that we have since adopted. It helps to foster an "ownership mentality," in contrast to the "entitlement mentality" that we see prevalent in the behavior of many employees at that level.

The company has a strong reputation for being very prudent and they teach this to their employees. I believe strongly that the company's culture of prudence is a major contributing factor to their success and attainment of market leadership. I remember a personal experience I had with the organization during a weekend program I facilitated for their HR department. On getting to the venue early to set up, I noticed that the lights came on but the Air-Cooling (AC) system stayed off.

To my amazement, when the delegates arrived, they opened the windows and sat down to commence the program. When I asked why the AC was not on (thinking it was faulty), I was told that it was the policy of the organization not to use the generator on weekends as a way of managing costs. It is only the CEO who could approve the usage of the generator on weekends. Without approval, the building was to operate on the uninterruptible (backup) power supply installed, which is not sufficient to run the air conditioners. The implication is that anybody working over the weekend has to make the sacrifice and endure a bit of discomfort.

That approach was life-transforming for me. I took the lessons and implemented them in my organization immediately.

Have a Powerful Employee Value Proposition (EVP)

Great candidates will be attracted by a powerful Employee Value Proposition (EVP). An EVP states what your organization offers an employee in return for their contributions. A strong one promotes your values and creates the unique qualities, perceptions, images, and experiences that attract talent. (A great EVP is also crucial for the retention of talent, but that's for another book!). An EVP answers the question, "Why should you come and work for us?"

Despite what many people believe, an EVP must describe much more than compensations and benefits. It must strike a fine balance between the tangible and intangible rewards received by employees. It must show what the organization expects in return. An EVP is everything that matters to employees about their work and their organization. It comprises the things they boast of at social gatherings.

The CIC Framework

On consulting assignments that involve helping organizations define and articulate their EVP, we use this framework to highlight the components that employees value:

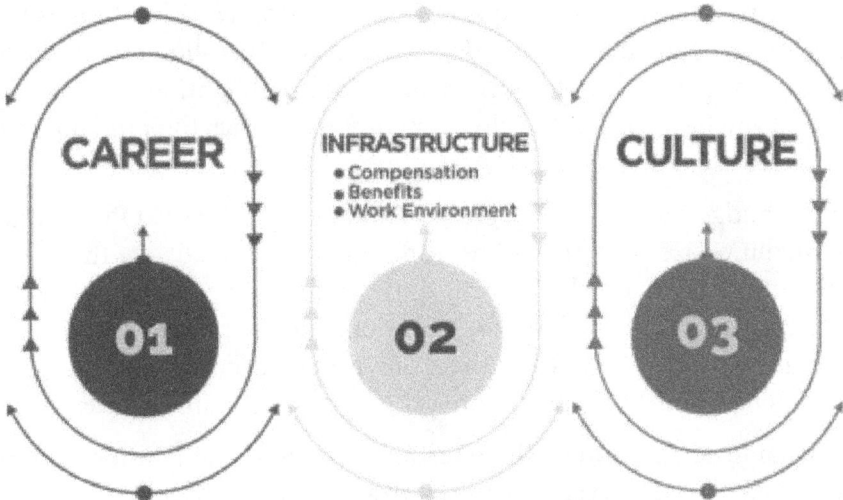

CAREER

INFRASTRUCTURE
- Compensation
- Benefits
- Work Environment

CULTURE

01 02 03

Career consists of job satisfaction and stability, chances to rise within the organization, learning and development opportunities, coaching & mentoring, evaluation and feedback mechanisms, and contribution to the work process. All of these add up to make a job rewarding and exciting.

Infrastructure refers to the frameworks, processes, and resources the organization provides to ensure the employee has a healthy work-life balance and is enabled to perform effectively and efficiently. This can be further subdivided into three broad categories:

a) *Compensation:* value, timeliness, and fairness of remuneration packages such as salary, bonuses, and promotions.

b) *Benefits:* a wide range of non-financial bonuses, which include paid time off (holidays, vacation, and sick days), family support, life, and health insurance, and retirement, tuition and disability benefits.

c) *Work Environment:* this includes organizational attributes: reputation for quality, clarity of roles and responsibilities, work autonomy, employee recognition system, and work tools.

Culture describes the norms, behaviors, ideals and social responsibilities of the organization. It is represented by trust, teamwork, and support between employees, their colleagues, and the management team.

EVP is the exact analogy of a product or corporate brand but for internal not external consumption. Just as you diligently and painstakingly invest time and resources in creating a powerful Customer Value Proposition (CVP), your Employee Value Proposition (EVP) should reflect the fundamental principles of your organization, highlighting who you are and what you have to offer to help your employees reach their full potential and deliver exceptional results

Size, budget, and industry greatly influence your EVP. Often, small- and medium-sized organizations differentiate by focusing their EVP on their provision of challenging and stimulating work in a flexible environment. In contrast, large organizations can offer their widely diverse career growth opportunities as the value proposition. Other factors that can influence your EVP content are geographic and cultural differences.

For large organizations, the question of having one EVP or multiple EVPs usually arises. Overall, an organization should have one principal EVP that applies to all of its employees. This can be further customized to reflect the requirements and preferences of key workforce segments such as core-skill employees, high potentials, and top performers.

Your EVP strategy must clearly demonstrate what you stand for and the benefits you promise to deliver. It must serve as a hard-to-duplicate competitive weapon. Many businesses are aware of this need, but the challenge lies (as usual) not in knowing but in doing. Vague words are often spoken, while the EVP remains clearly undefined and unarticulated.

Alternatively, in some organizations the EVP has been established and articulated, but still fails to grab the attention of talented candidates out there (or the existing workforce). There can be various reasons for this:

- The attributes are not business/stakeholder relevant
- The EVP is undifferentiated and does not stand out from competitors'
- The EVP is inconsistent with business realities
- Once created, the EVP is not adequately integrated into the company's policies and practices. It remains theoretical, like a mission statement hanging on a wall that nobody really believes in or follows.

It is imperative to know how to define, articulate, hone, communicate, embed, and implement a compelling, realistic, and effective EVP for your organization.

CASE STUDY

Creating a Compelling EVP

In the description of how EVP is put into practice, I will describe a consultancy project my firm carried out for a Fast-Moving Consumer Goods (FMCG) company. The brief was to help solve the problem of finding and retaining the right employees.

The company was faced with many challenges. Advances in technology coupled with globalization, as well as geopolitical and economic forces, were transforming many of its clients' consumer habits day-by-day. The startling number of alternatives and the unpredictable customer base meant that the company had to build agile teams. However, the human capital needed to achieve that was not available in the right quantity within the organization.

In the course of carrying out our initial diagnostics, we discovered that the company faced an overall shortage of qualified applicants and had no long-term strategy for maintaining a pool of top talents. The only way to achieve this target was to improve its image as an employer.

We had the company carry out an Employee Engagement Survey, asking four questions:

1. What are we currently doing that is good enough to be continued?

2. What are we doing that needs to be improved?

3. How can the organization improve and reinforce the good?

4. How can the organization improve in poor areas?

We carried out exit interviews and ran focus groups. Between them, these diagnostics revealed several key issues, including communication, favoritism, and career growth opportunities.

We then worked with top management on how to make improvements in these areas, and put these improvements at the heart of how the business was run. We also worked them into a set of simple slogans and images and made sure that all the business' stakeholders became aware of them.

Finally, we suggested the company set up a Staff Advisory Board, a group of seven employees with one team lead, in charge of driving implementation and enforcement of the new policies. They also had a mandate to keep looking for ways of improving the EVP.

The company acted on our suggestion.

At the end of the program, the feedback was excellent, surprising even us. By the end of the first year after the development and implementation of the EVP, the company had improved employee engagement by a factor of five and witnessed significant improvements in its financial performance.

Every organization has an EVP, whether it is formalized and written down or not. Every activity in the employee lifecycle contributes to an informal and inadvertent EVP. Rather than leaving it to chance, it is much better to develop an EVP that aligns with your target audience consciously. Such an EVP will guide and strengthen your employer branding efforts in the talent market while attracting the best fit for your organizational objectives.

For more information on this topic, visit **www.hiringrightbook.com** to download the complete guide to creating and developing your EVP.

Always Keep Searching and Hiring

Whenever it comes to my knowledge that a company has put a freeze on hiring, I'm always concerned. While I understand the circumstances under which a company will do this, I don't believe this should be implemented strictly in every role across every area of the organization. Organizations must always be searching for and hiring the right employees for those roles upon which the successful execution of the company strategy hinges.

Companies must always be sourcing for suitable candidates for their mission-critical roles. Even if you have capable people in these roles today, anything can happen. Take the example of McDonald's, which lost two CEOs in the space of six months. If they had not had a healthy succession plan in place, it could have been highly damaging to the business.

My firm has partnered with companies in the past to help them identify successors to their critical roles even when those roles have incumbents. These organizations fundamentally understand that it is already too late to start searching after receiving a quit notice from an employee in a critical role. We help these organizations source, identify, and start building relationships with candidates who can be potential successors for their critical roles as a backup plan (it is referred to as having an external succession plan).

Having the successor in another organization only makes sense as a Plan C and should be treated accordingly. Plan A is to do whatever it takes to hold on to your very best people. Plan B is to have a solid succession plan in place within your organization with successors who are ready to step up within six to twelve months. Plan C is to proactively identify and cultivate relationships with potential successors in other organizations.

Do You Know Your Actual Competitors?

Whenever I ask HR professionals or executives who their competitors are, they usually respond by sharing the names of their traditional rivals who offer the same products and services to the same set of customers in the same industry. Sometimes they go a little further and identify providers of substitutes. Unfortunately, this is grossly inadequate and represents a major blind spot.

Nowadays, your competitors are any and all organizations that can poach your talent (or from whom you can do the same). It doesn't matter how big they are, where they are, or what their product/service is: If they can attract your best people and if you can hire the "right fit" employees from them, they are your competitors.

This is both good and bad. The good thing is that you can expand your talent pool to include a wider list of targeted organizations to attract talent from. The bad thing is that companies/institutions that are not even on your radar can lure away your best people, and it is very little you can do about it except to be aware of the possibility.

The biggest competition that organizations in my business environment are facing in the area of talent is that of migration to countries like Canada. My company and many of our clients have experienced significant talent losses to this behemoth competitor.

So what can you do, in the face of this challenge?

Look at Potential and Transferable Skills

When the exact skill set is nowhere to be found in your pool of applicants, you will need to get creative about how you vet candidates. It is highly beneficial to focus on soft skills and transferable skills. Candidates may not have experience or training, but that doesn't mean they don't have potential. With your guidance, you can mold green recruits into some of your most effective employees.

For example, if you see on their résumé that they taught themselves how to use a certain type of software, it doesn't matter if you don't use that software in your business. The takeaway is that they are self-starting, fast-learning, and likely to pick up your company's software and processes quickly.

Outsource

This is one aspect of globalization that you can easily take advantage of. If you can't find local talent to work for your company, it's time to cast a wider net. Contract and freelance workers are becoming more commonplace. According to Forbes, the share of the U.S. workforce in the gig economy rose from 10.1 percent in 2005 to 15.8 percent in 2015. That trend has continued.

In addition to securing the talent your business needs to flourish, you can enjoy other benefits of outsourcing: keeping overheads down. You don't need to pay benefits to contract workers, and you only need to pay them for the work they do rather than have someone on the payroll full-time.

Protect Your Reputation

Whatever the circumstances, it is never wise to burn bridges with employees. Although you can't stop anyone from walking out the door and going to the competition, you never know when that talent may choose to come back.

As the old adage goes, the grass is not always greener on the other side. If you're able to affably part ways with your previous employees, they won't hesitate to ask for their job back if things don't turn out as they had hoped with your competitor.

On the other hand, a disgruntled ex-employee can make a lot of noise about a negative experience with your company. This can drive talent away. Do things by the book and protect your brand's reputation!

Build a Succession Plan

Senior employees may be winding down their careers, but that doesn't mean they need to quit your company "cold turkey." If you have an older employee who has started talking about retirement, ask them if they're open to taking their retirement in phases over a few months or years.

This can be arranged in a way that is agreeable to both of you, like working fewer days or hours per week. A phased retirement helps both the retiree and your company to gradually adjust to the change. It is also a good stress test for your younger employees who will be picking up the slack during the times your retiring employee is not in.

Get Feedback – Then Use It

Ask your current employees what they like about the company and what could be improved. Although you can do this with one-on-one meetings, it is wise to provide more anonymous options as well, like an employee survey through a third party or a suggestion box.

Employees are seldom honest to your face about the things that really irk them about the company (or about you!). Providing an outlet for anonymous feedback makes them feel comfortable that they can be truthful about both the good and the bad.

If an employee has resigned, make sure you conduct an exit interview and ask questions about why they are leaving.

Of course, it's not enough to just listen to feedback. Use that feedback to identify your employees' main pain points about working for your company. Then take whatever remedial measures are necessary.

The talent shortage is real and it's probably going to get worse before it gets better. But being aware of what it is and why it's happening can help you become part of the solution. It is up to each organization to do its part in educating, training, and growing the current workforce and the upcoming generation. Your business can still thrive in adversity. Be strategic about finding, keeping and creating talent, and business will continue to flourish.

KEY TAKEAWAYS

- It is a competitive talent market out there because the demand for the right people far outweighs the supply. The very best know their worth and will make employment decisions in the light of that.

- This is especially true outside the developed world, where there is a perpetual threat of a "brain drain."

- The problem is exacerbated further by falling educational standards, which makes finding the right people even more difficult.

- Millennials, while technologically savvy, often lack "soft skills."

- However, all is not lost!

- Smart companies pay over the odds for quality.

- They develop their own talent internally.

- They have a compelling Employee Value Proposition, which they put into practice as well as preach, and which they broadcast to the world.

- They keep searching for good people, even when they have no pressing need to. Never stop searching for the right fit people for your organization. Never!

- Protect your reputation.

- Be aware of your rivals in the "war for talent." There are more than you think, as your competition in the talent market is much wider than your competition in the product markets where you operate.

- Complement your talent pool by outsourcing some functions to contract and feelance talent.

CHAPTER TEN

THE POWER OF MURPHY'S LAW

"If there's any way to do it wrong, he will find it."
Captain Edward A Murphy

Murphy's Law was born at Edwards Air Force Base, California, in 1949. It was named after Captain Edward A. Murphy, an engineer working on a project to study how much sudden deceleration a person could withstand in an aircraft crash. (The project gifted the world the seat belt that we now use in cars. It also made its leader, Colonel John P. Stapp, "the fastest man in the world," frequently accelerating him to more than 600 mph on a rocket-powered sled.)

Legend has it that one day, after finding that a transducer had been wired wrongly, Murphy cursed the technician responsible, adding, "If there is any way to do it wrong, he will find it." Colonel Stapp had a habit of keeping notes about anything he found unusual or interesting, and wrote this down, calling it Murphy's Law. Over time, he added other versions of the same thought. All of these versions are now referred to as Murphy's Law. Below are some of my all-time favorites:

1. If anything can go wrong, it will
2. If there's a probability of several things going wrong, the one that will cause the most damage will be the first one to go wrong
3. If nothing can go wrong, something will anyway
4. If you perceive that there are four possible ways in which something can go wrong and circumvent these, then a fifth way will promptly develop
5. Left to themselves, things tend to go from bad to worse
6. If everything seems to be going well, you have obviously overlooked something

When it comes to hiring right, years of experience have taught me that this law is real. Not everyone agrees: I remember when I first shared the concept with a colleague of mine who insisted that there was no such thing and that I must have invented it because of how paranoid I was. It took only a Google search to convince him that I hadn't created Murphy's Law!

What has Murphy's Law got to do with Hiring Right?

The answer is EVERYTHING.

When it comes to running a successful organization and hiring right, the best thing you can do is to let this law guide you. Despite our very best efforts, we can still get it wrong, and there is no room for anything less than the best shots. Absolutely no room. I know this from my personal experience and the near-death encounters my business has had from not considering these laws.

If hiring right is indeed a matter of life and death for the organization—and it definitely is—then anything short of anticipating Murphy's Law and putting in place measures to prevent its occurrence will simply not do.

I always encourage business executives, hiring managers, and HR professionals to be "productively paranoid" when it comes to hiring employees into their organizations.

Many people tend to view being paranoid as a negative thing. It is negative if the paranoia renders you helpless, takes away your self-belief, or makes you lose hope and stop trying. That is why what I am proposing is *Productive Paranoia*—the type that motivates you to act proactively in preparation for the unknown.

Productive paranoia has the potential to galvanize you into action. It makes you put in place all possible measures to ensure things go according to plan. It makes you think outside the box and consider alternative options to ensure you're not leaving things to chance. This is crucial to ongoing success, in life and in business.

When hiring top people, this mentality is essential. Go through all the formalities and the structured assessments but also assume that somehow these systems might be flawed.

Speak to people, off the record, as suggested in Chapter Six. Don't stop doing this until you have a clear picture in your mind of the person, as they really are. If you still think they're the right hire, take them on, but if doubts emerge, don't. Hiring right is just too important!

CASE STUDY

Productive Paranoia

We had built a splendid new office facility and decided to have a proper opening ceremony for it. We managed to secure the ex-president of the country to preside over this event.

My Productive Paranoia kicked in: What could go wrong?

One thing I particularly worried about was loss of power (a not uncommon event in the city where we were based). I told the team organizing the event to hire a stand-by generator just in case, and they told me that the building had two brand new generators already.

I told them to hire a third one, just in case. They looked at me strangely but did as I said.

Needless to say, on the afternoon of the event, there was a power outage—and the two existing generators failed to kick in.

When the stakes are high, don't leave anything to chance!

If it's too good to be true, it's probably not true, and it's likely not good.

Have you experienced a situation where you hired a fantastic candidate, and then a completely different employee shows up for work on the resumption day?

Well, the same individual physically but different in every other sense - attitude, behavior, work ethics, competence, etc.

I have encountered this situation several times in the past, and upon a detailed review of the root cause, the gaps unearthed more often than not occurred at the selection stage. Sadly, these gaps could have been avoided by implementing a well-designed recruitment process.

From my personal experience, candidates that end up performing underwhelmingly on the job even though they had ticked all the right boxes during the selection process are usually very articulate, confident, well-coordinated, and interview exceptionally well.

Their well-orchestrated performance at the interview can cause the interviewer/assessor to overlook crucial gaps. You, the hiring manager, will do well to serve your organization's objective by exercising caution when interviewing such candidates. Like the popular saying of millennials, "it's all packaging."

Below are warning signs you should be acutely aware of;

1. If, based on your assessment and their demonstrated competence during the hiring process, they should ideally be further ahead in their career and earning significantly more than they currently do, be careful. Do not get carried away, thinking you are getting someone great on the cheap. If it is too good to be true...

2. If they have been let go by a previous employer. Truly, some candidates experience unfortunate circumstances in their former places of employment, and this shouldn't count against them in any way. My second best hire of all times was let go from her previous organization for a reason that had nothing to do with her character or competence; my phenomenal gain at the end of the day. You must exercise due diligence and check that the candidate in question was not disengaged because of gaps in their character and competence. This is so important.

3. If there are several unexplained gaps in their CV. A client once hired a brilliant graphic artist who would just disappear for a week; phones off, emails down, completely unreachable, only to reappear with the most bizarre of excuses. One time, he alleged that he had been kidnapped, but no ransom demand had been made. My client kept accepting his excuses because he was unbelievably good until his attitude started affecting the morale of the rest of the team, and clients' projects began to suffer. A retrospective look at his CV revealed several unexplained gaps that should have put my client on inquiry.

4. If the candidate moves jobs too frequently. Some candidates are just restless. And because they interview extremely well, there will always

be an interested employer. It is the name of the game. You must beware of such candidates as they can cause loss of momentum and disruption to your business, especially if they are handling major clients or occupying a critical role.

All the signs described above do not necessarily have adverse outcomes. For every rule, there are exceptions, and I have encountered several variations of the above signs over the years to know that we shouldn't stereotype candidates based on them. Having said this, I have, however, also made enough hiring mistakes to realize that these issues are areas of potential future problems, and those charged with the responsibility of making hiring decisions should mind these gaps.

Some of these wrongly hired candidates have turned out to have severe productivity-limiting deficiencies that are very difficult to discover during a full-blown assessment center exercise.

Hiring individuals where the story doesn't add up is too risky and almost always never ends very well. Be productively paranoid!

KEY TAKEAWAYS

- Professionals don't leave things to chance.
- When it comes to hiring right, Murphy's Law is real and must be factored into the whole process.
- Productive Paranoia is the key to galvanizing yourself into action to ensure you succeed despite all odds.
- If it is too good to be true, it is probably not good, and probably not true.

CONCLUSION

"Get the right people on the bus and the wrong people off the bus."

Jim Collins

The old adage that "people are your greatest asset" is a dangerous oversimplification. People who are not the right fit for your organization can be your greatest liability.

I say this rather than "the wrong people can be your greatest liability" because, in my over twenty years of work experience, I've yet to come across a "wrong person." However, unfortunately, I have come across hundreds of "wrong fits." Hiring is context-sensitive and "fit" is the most crucial consideration. Most employees labeled as "wrong people" will thrive and succeed phenomenally in some other context (even sometimes within the same organization).

I believe it is the ultimate responsibility of organizations to ensure they implement robust, structured, and rigorous hiring processes and practices geared toward ensuring that only candidates that are a fit for the organizational context are hired.

If you make the wrong hire, you're in serious trouble and all the revolutionary management techniques in the world won't save you. No management system or principle in the world can make up for hiring less than the best talent for your organization.

The good news is that hiring right is usually the best solution to an organization's problems. Sixty to seventy percent of the success of your organization—maybe more—will be determined by the amount and quality of talent that you have. It is great people who spot new opportunities, great people who generate extra revenue, great people who develop the ideas, technologies, systems and, most important of all, the other people who will drive the business.

Hiring right is an organization's best chance of surviving and thriving. It should never be left to chance. Implementing a consistent process to unearth the right hire will always be worth the extra time and cost involved.

Luckily, over the years, I have learned the basics of this, and I hope this book has presented them all in a clear, convincing manner. As a quick reminder, they are…

The importance of context (see the comments about right and wrong "fits" above).

The need for well-thought-through, documented, standard hiring processes, which everyone in the organization knows, understands and follows.

The need to understand what success at a role really involves, and to replicate that in a Success Profile, so that when new incumbents for that role are needed, they can be selected in the light of that understanding and trained in any aspects of it where they need to be.

The need for anyone involved in the hiring process to understand its importance and for them to be trained in both the company's processes and general hiring skills.

The need for everyone involved in hiring to understand and overcome both their own personal 'Bias Codes' and those kinds of bias that are "hard-wired" into even the most fair-minded individual.

The importance of having a range of assessment tools, and not just relying on interviews, which can be "gamed" by smart candidates and which are particularly susceptible to bias and the candidate's propensity for overrating their own ability.

The proper checking of references is particularly important. With major decisions, informal chats with former bosses, co-workers or subordinates can be of particular value.

Managers must be made accountable for their hiring decisions. For this to happen, Hiring Right should be one of the KPIs of anyone given this responsibility. The best measure for this is the performance of a hire six months or a year after they have joined the organization. There is no short cut!

Resources must be made available for the hiring process to proceed smoothly and effectively. These include obvious things like buying proper psychometric systems and paying for decent settings for interviews (particularly important when interviewing for senior positions). More subtle issues, such as allowing busy managers time to prepare for rounds of interviews matter too.

Be prepared to pay over the odds for the best people.

Grow your own talent. The best hires can be internal ones.

Have a compelling Employee Value Proposition (EVP)—an answer to the question that every good potential employee asks: "Why should I come and work for you?" This must be compelling but also authentic. It is not a slogan; it is how you really do business and how you really treat your people (and, actually, how you treat all your stakeholders).

Always keep your eyes on the talent market.

Last but not least, remember Murphy's Law: If something can go wrong, it will. Don't let this get you down, but do let it make you "productively paranoid." The result should be more happiness, not less. Think of your nation's ex-president attending a function of yours, and two power generators failing—and how good it will feel as the extra one that you hired, against all advice, clicks into action and saves the day.

My hope and wish are for every business to become excellent at hiring right. I believe the positive difference this will make in the world will be immeasurable.

Wishing you phenomenal success in your business and life journey!

Hiring Practices Scorecard

Now that you have gone through the book and hopefully started implementing some of the recommendations, you can use this tool again to evaluate where you are on your journey to improving the effectiveness of your hiring processes and practices.

Visit www.hiringrightbook.com to download the Hiring Scorecard Template

Key:

1 = Not at all
2 = To a small extent
3 = Somewhat
4 = To a large extent
5 = To a very great extent

1	We carry out detailed analysis of our organisational context and realities to determine the strategic implications on roles we are hiring for.	1 2 3 4 5
2	We have well developed Success Profiles for our critical roles and we deploy them as guides as part of our hiring activities.	1 2 3 4 5
3	We have clearly defined and documented hiring processes and practices that everyone with a hiring responsibility is required to follow diligently.	1 2 3 4 5
4	All our Hiring Managers, Recruiters, Interviewers and HR Staff are well trained and certified on our hiring processes and practices.	1 2 3 4 5
5	We recognise the potential negative impact of biases on our hiring activities and we have put in place adequate practices to eliminate biases, as much as possible, in our hiring practices.	1 2 3 4 5
6	We deploy a variety of candidate selection methodologies (at least 3) as part of our hiring process to increase our chances of hiring right.	1 2 3 4 5
7	We have set standards and metrics and we hold our hiring personnel accountable to them.	1 2 3 4 5
8	We provide adequate resources (budget, space, people, time) for all our hiring activities to ensure we get it right.	1 2 3 4 5
9	We have a strategy and implementation plan in place to grow our own talent to reduce the impact of talent shortage on our business.	1 2 3 4 5
10	We recognise that despite our best efforts, we can still experience failure in hiring right so we are productively paranoid and we do not leave anything to chance when it comes to our hiring process and practices.	1 2 3 4 5

Total Score: _____

Scoring Instructions: Add up the numeric value (1 to 5) of all the selected boxes. The maximum possible score is 50. Use the table below to assess the readiness of your hiring team to deliver the right people to support your business strategy and aspirations.

Points	Assessment Result
>45	Excellent likelihood of Hiring Right. Action: Continue a disciplined approach to improving your hiring practices; strengthen lowest-scoring items.
33-44	Moderate likelihood for hiring right, but results may be less than optimal. Action: Strengthen weakest items to raise the score to > 44.
<32	Hiring Right is less likely. Action: Urgently overhaul your entire hiring processes and practices in a systemic way.

Tools for Your Hiring Journey

You can't build a world-class organization without a world-class hiring practice. Get the right tools and resources to support you at **www.hiringrightbook.com** now.

Article Library

Tips, techniques and real best practice examples with action steps you can apply right away. Learn what you can do right now to improve your hiring practices and processes to build a world-class organization.

Assessment

How effective is your hiring practice? Use the hiring practices scorecard tool to evaluate the effectiveness of your hiring processes and practices.

Online Courses

Our online courses explain how the hiring right principles work, and how you can utilize and implement it for your organization right away. Each course is packed with case study examples, insights, and results. You can learn more online, anytime, anywhere, at your convenience.

Quotations on Hiring

Hundreds of quotations on hiring right from the author, Bolaji Olagunju, and other famous people. Enjoy and share these words of wisdom.

Join the Hiring Right Community

Join Bolaji Olagunju and many other business owners and executives with enthusiasm and belief in hiring right, sharing the latest news, ideas, discussions, inspirations and advice. Get answers to your questions, and advice from around the world to solve your hiring problems. Share the Hiring Right book with your friends, colleagues, bosses, and business owners. Help eradicate bad hiring practices and increase the probability of organizational success.

Email Newsletter

Subscribing to the newsletter service is the best way of keeping in touch. You will receive free articles, videos, white papers, and other valuable tools for improving your hiring practices and building a world-class organization.

Blog

The blog is an open community for committed business owners, executives and HR professionals. We are dedicated to building enduring businesses.

LinkedIn

If you are a business owner, business executive, head of HR, senior leader or manager responsible for hiring people for your organization, you can connect with Bolaji Olagunju through the world's largest professional networking community.

Facebook

Be a fan of Hiring Right Book on Facebook. Like this page to enjoy all the latest news, photographs, and updates.

Twitter

Follow on Twitter for instant updates on what's happening, including tips, insights and ideas for hiring right.

ABOUT THE AUTHOR

Bolaji Olagunju is a serial entrepreneur, angel investor, marketing enthusiast, coach, mentor, and consultant to some of the most interesting businesses in Africa.

With over 20 years of experience in the areas of human resources, business management, sales & marketing, he has been privileged to have worked on major organizational development and transformation projects across several industries.

He is an alumnus of London Business School and has attended several programs in leading universities all over the world including Berkeley Haas School of Business, Colombia business school, Michigan Ross business school, Kellogg business school and UNC Kenan- Flagler business school.

Early mornings are his best time in the day. Seek him out and you will be sure to find him in his UK/Nigerian home or office, surrounded by towering tomes from the greats. His best authors since 2004 still remains Jim Collins and Dave Ulrich.

He is deeply passionate about learning, teaching, and mentoring young entrepreneurs while creating avenues to improve employability and job opportunities across Africa.

And he has personally conducted over 10,000 job interviews and trained more than 50 000 people on varied business principles and skills.

Bolaji is the founder, Workforce Group (**www.workforcegroup.com**), a group of professional services firms with a focus on business advisory, learning & development, outsourcing, recruitment & assessment, market entry & operations support, etc.

A co-founder in several technology start-ups including Peerless (an e-learning management system), Outwork (a task management solution), AllDay HR (a Human Resource Software for large corporations and SMEs) and Maudition (an innovative video application designed purely for entertainment, yep!).

And owner of The Zone (**www.thezone.ng**), a world-class purpose-built facility suitable for meetings, training, conferences, retreats, strategy sessions, team building events, virtual offices, biometric centers, research sessions, and corporate events. As well as Zone Tech Park, a venture builder for ideas generated by the rockstar in-house teams, and for external clients & corporates looking to execute a project.

What did you think of this book?

I am really keen to hear from you about this book, so that I can continue to improve on it.

Please log on to the following website and leave me your feedback.

It will only take a few minutes and your thoughts are invaluable to me.

www.hiringrightbook.com/bookfeedback

HIRING BRIEF QUESTIONNAIRE

Date: _____

General Information

Company Name: _____

Job Role: _____

Reports to: _____

No of Vacant Positions: _____

Locations: _____

Interview Location: _____

What backgrounds should the ideal candidates have (e.g., candidates who have worked in X industry or Y company managing multiple projects and supervising a large team be an added advantage)?

_____

_____

_____

_____

Is there any organization/industry you would particularly like us to target?

_____

_____

_____

_____

What challenges have you had with recruiting for similar roles in the past?

_____

_____

_____

_____

Person Specification

Personality of ideal candidate:

_____

Age Limit: _____

Gender:　　Male ☐　　Female ☐　　Both ☐

Years of experience: _____

Employment type/Duration of service: _____

Qualification(s): _____

Positive indicators: _____

_____

_____

Negative indicators (what sort of candidates will not be a fit): _____

_____

_____

_____

Recruiting Information

Competences required for the Job, e.g.:

☐ Candidate with strong analytical disposition

☐ Excellent administrative skills

☐ Excellent communication skills (oral & written)

☐ Good presentation skills

_____

_____

Key Responsibilities/Targets (if any):

_____

_____

Please give us three interview type/screening questions (technical)—and the answers/your expectations—so that we can screen short-listed candidates more effectively?

a) Question: _____

_____

Answer: _____

_____

b) Question: _____

_____

Answer: _____

_____

c) Question: _____

_____

Answer: _____

_____

Remuneration

Gross salary range: _____

Annual package: _____ Monthly Package: _____

Benefits: _____

What are the top four to five non-negotiable criteria without which the ideal candidate cannot excel in the target role?

_____

_____

_____

Additional information:

_____

_____

Acknowledgements:

I acknowledge that the information above captures the requirement of the role.

For:..

Name: _____

Designation: _____

Signature/Date: _____

For: Workforce Group: ....

Name: _____

Designation: _____

Signature/Date: _____

Stay Interview Template

Questions	Responses
What do you enjoy most about your work?	
Are there some aspects of your job that you would like to change or improve?	
What do you see as your top three strengths? Are you utilizing them often in your work?	
What do you need to get better at and how would that impact your performance in your current job?	
How can I help you improve and achieve your career goals?	
Is there any reason why this is not the right place for you or reason/s why you might leave?	
Do you have any suggestions for me?